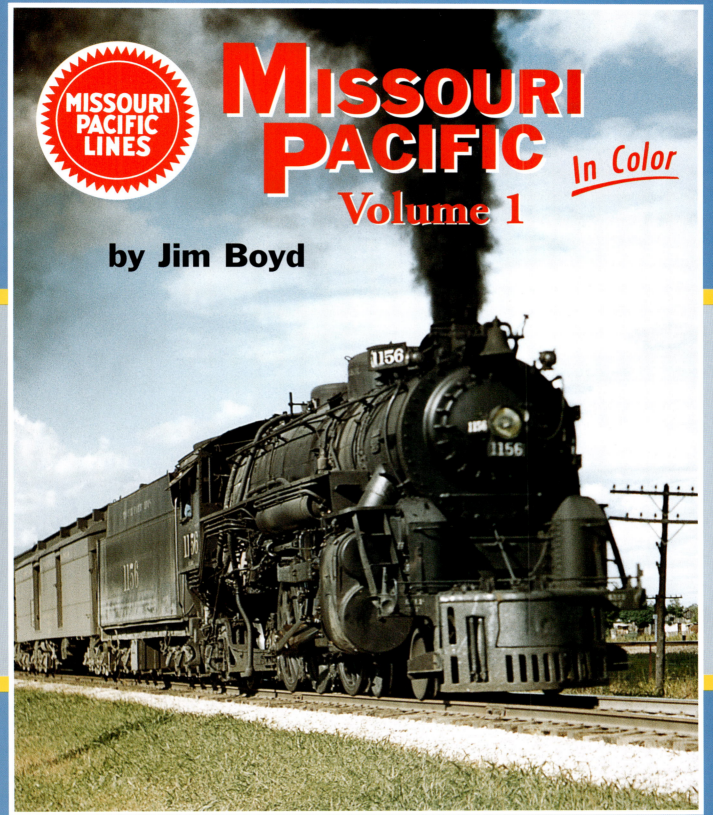

Missouri Pacific Volume 1

In Color

by Jim Boyd

ST. LOUIS, Brownsville & Mexico 4-6-2 1156 was on the *Sunshine Special* at San Marcos, Texas, in August 1946.

The Era of the *Eagles*

Copyright © 2004
Morning Sun Books, Inc.
All rights reserved. This book may not be reproduced in part or in whole without written permission from the publisher, except in the case of brief quotations or reproductions of the cover for the purpose of review.

Published by
Morning Sun Books, Inc.
9 Pheasant Lane
Scotch Plains, NJ 07076

Library of Congress
Catalog Card No. 93-078207

First Printing
ISBN 1-58248-133-4

Book design and layout by Jim Boyd

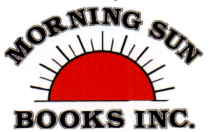

Logos used under Union Pacific license.

Printed in Korea

Dedication

WALT GROSSELFINGER of Middletown, New Jersey, was very helpful in gathering material for this book. We have been friends for more than 30 years through our mutual friendship with the late Don Ball. Walt has been the very responsible trustee of Don's photo collection and has made valuable images available for quite a number of Morning Sun Books projects.

In addition, Walt has been a driving force in large scale historical projects, including the groundwork for the creation of a new Jersey State Transportation Museum that is still struggling its way through the state legislature. Walt's love of steam locomotives and railroading in general have been shared with thousands of others through his promoting of the historic recreation of N.J. Transit's two-tone green "Erie" E8s and the restoration of the New York Central 20th Century Limited observation lounge car Hickory Creek. An excellent photographer, Walt was expressing his delight (right) with the photo he'd just gotten of Ross Rowland's C&O 4-8-4 on coal train tests at Handley, West Virginia, in January 1985.

JIM BOYD

Acknowledgements

THE AUTHOR would like to thank the following people for their contributions to this book: Publisher Bob Yanosey conceived the project and offered me the opportunity to edit the wonderful array of photos that he had gathered for it, including the extensive material from Emery Gulash, Matt Herson, Al Holtz, T.J. McNamara, Mac Owen and Lou Schmitz. Special thanks go to Louis A. Marre and A. Dean Hale for their significant contributions to the project and their quick response to my requests for specific subjects. Thanks also go to Jim Ogden, president of the Missouri Pacific Historical Society (www.mopac.org).

This book would have been impossible without the contributions of the following photographers: Peter Arnold, Don Ball, Bob's Photos, Steve Bogen, R.L. Borcherding, John Brunner, R.H. Carlson, Marvin H. Cohen, Robert F. Collins, W. Dance, R. Fillman, David Graeff, Walt Grosselfinger, Robert Hegge, J. David Ingles, Ray Lowry, Charles Mizell Jr., Jim Neubauer, Dr. Art Peterson, Gaylord Plummer, R.S. Plummer, Alan Ramsey, Dick Rumholz, R.L. Schmidt, Jim Seacrest, Bill G. Sharp, Greg C. Sieren, Don Simms, Stuart J. Sutton, Richard R. Wallin and Bob Yanosey.

The primary reference sources were Kevin EuDaly's *Missouri Pacific Diesel Power* (White River Productions, 1994), Joe Collias' *Mopac Power* (Howell-North Books, 1980) and George Drury's *Historical Guide to North American Railroads* (Kalmbach Publishing Co., 1985) and *Guide to North American Steam Locomotives* (Kalmbach Publishing Co., 1993) and *Extra 2200 South*.

Sig Gulash

As this book was in preparation in late February 2004, Sig Gulash, the wife of Emery Gulash, passed away at their home in Dearborn, Michigan. As Emery's health had begun to deteriorate over the last few years, Sig became his caregiver and was very helpful in making sure his photo collection was put into good hands. The Emery Gulash collection is now the property of Morning Sun Books, where we are fulfilling Emery's desire to have his lifelong photographic efforts shared with others.

Between Black and Blue

FOREWORD

MISSOURI PACIFIC PHOTO

A PERFECTLY MATCHED A-B-A SET of E7s posed against the Front Range for the company photographer in 1948 on the *Colorado Eagle* in the blue and gray livery that Raymond Loewy had created for the pioneer St. Louis-Omaha *Eagle* in 1940.

THE RAILROAD that we think of today as "the Missouri Pacific" was created in the first quarter of the 20th Century when the lines west of St. Louis were joined by 1924 with the St. Louis, Iron Mountain & Southern to Texarkana and the Gulf Coast Lines from New Orleans to Houston and Laredo. Because of Texas incorporation laws, many of the predecessor companies survived into the 1950s (see *Capsule History*, **page 122**).

The president of the newly unified Missouri Pacific Lines was Lewis W. Baldwin, who had declared in 1923 that "the only proper color for a steam locomotive is black." Thus the MoPac steamed into the mid-20th Century with black engines adorned with silver lettering and a minimum of frivolity.

On January 16, 1961, Downing B. Jenks became president of the Missouri Pacific, and he decreed, to paraphrase Mr. Baldwin, that "the only proper color for a diesel locomotive is dark blue," with white ScotchLite and a minimum of frivolity. The entire system diesel fleet was soon wearing the economical but surprisingly attractive "Jenks blue."

Between the Baldwin black and Jenks blue, however, the Missouri Pacific and its wayward kin in Texas and Oklahoma had a colorful era of *Eagle* streamliners and uniform freight power as diesels displaced steam. The MoPac was a modern but modest railroad, struggling through the industry's longest bankruptcy, 23 years from 1933 to 1956. Its handful of handsome 4-8-4s was vastly outnumbered by World War I vintage Pacifics, Mikados and 4-8-2s, as well as a supporting cast of Consolidations and Ten-Wheelers. Its brand new *Eagle* streamliner of 1940 was a dazzler of the prewar era, styled by no less than the renowned Raymond Loewy. While the early diesel switchers followed President Baldwin's black edict, the General Motors Styling Section picked up Loewy's *Eagle* blue theme and applied it to the wartime FT freight units. The diesels that replaced steam in the next decade were modest and conservative designs with a minimum of frivolity.

This book covers that Era of the *Eagles* from the end of steam through the first generation diesels to the system renumbering of 1962. The Texas & Pacific is included as a separate chapter, and its diesels are handled separately in the production tallies.

Because the MoPac dieselized comparatively early, color steam photography is scarce. Morning Sun Books had available Emery Gulash's remarkable coverage of the Texas lines in the mid-1940s, that conveys the "feel" of the MoPac steam era. I just wish the Army Air Corps would have also assigned him to someplace closer to Kirkwood Hill so he could have done equal justice to those 4-8-4s!

JIM BOYD
CRANDON LAKES, N.J.
FEBRUARY 20, 2004

Contents

FOREWORD / 3   INTRODUCTION / 5

CHAPTER 1
Emery in Texas, 1945 / 6
Texas Pacifics / 8   Brownsville Mikes / 13   Texas Ten-Wheelers / 20
Miscellaneous Power / 24   Switching to with Stam / 26

CHAPTER 2
Diesels and *Eagles* / 28
Hatching an *Eagle* / 30   The *Eagle* Takes Flight / 32
Doodlebugs and the *Eaglet* / 38   The *Eagle* at Jefferson City / 40
More E's and More *Eagles* / 42   EMD's FT: Wartime Freight Diesels / 48
The F3 Fleet / 50   Covered Wagons from Schenectady / 52
A Handful of Hermaphrodites / 56   The Unique F5s / 56   Babyfaces / 58
More Power: F7s and E8s / 60   Alcos for the *Eagles* / 63
Black Switchers / 66   Geeps / 70   Alco FA2s / 72
Baldwin AS16s and Alco RS3s / 76   Last of the First Generation / 78
Eagle Merchandise Service / 80
Grand Avenue Junction: September 11, 1960 / 82

CHAPTER 3
The Texas & Pacific / 84
Steam on the Texas & Pacific / 86   Swamp Holly Orange / 88
T&P Switchers – Orange and Otherwise / 90
Variations on an *Eagle* / 92   The Midland Valley / 94

CHAPTER 4
Jenks Blue / 100
New Colors / Old Numbers / 102   Old Colors / New Numbers / 104
Transition in Texas and Oklahoma / 110
A Second-Hand E8 / 112   Jenks Blue with a Different Slant / 114
The Amazing "Mike & Ike" / 116   Blue Alco Road Switchers / 118
Missouri Pacific Capsule History / 122   Rosters and Map / 123
Epilogue: Preview "Screamin' Eagles" / 128

LOUIS A. MARRE

DON BALL COLLECTION

Introduction

THE EAGLE DOMAIN

THE MISSOURI PACIFIC was just another railroad at St. Louis Union Station when I got my first good look at it in 1965. In 1968, however, my job with EMD often got me into Texarkana, where I could observe it much more closely. The "MOP and TP" held my interest even compared to the nearby Cotton Belt and Kansas City Southern. As I write this, beside my computer is an HO scale model of the streamlined sleeper *Eagle Domain*, painted by Texarkanian Bill Sharp. The very "sound" of that name still sums up the appeal of the Missouri Pacific to me.

CLASSIC IMAGES of the MoPac's first generation diesel era are represented (above) by the A-B-B-B-A set of F-units led by boiler-equipped F3 566, at Van Buren, Ark., on August 13, 1960, and (opposite) the system's first E7, 7004, heading up the domeliner *Missouri River Eagle* at Leavenworth, Kansas, on December 27, 1952.

5

Emery in Texas, 1945

CHAPTER ONE

EMERY GULASH of Dearborn, Michigan, had a lifelong fascination with trains, airplanes and ships (in that order) and captured them all on film. He was born in Lansing in February 1918 and later worked as a draftsman for General Motors at Dearborn. He began taking 35mm color slides in 1941, and at the beginning of the Second World War, he and his friend Hal Jackson were in the Civil Air Patrol. In 1943 he joined the Army Air Corps as a lieutenant and navigator.

Emery spent most of 1945 at San Marcos, Texas, on the International-Great Northern Laredo-Longview main line, the route of the heavyweight St. Louis-Mexico City *Sunshine Special*. In early 1946 he was assigned to Ellington Field in Olcott, Texas, 15 miles below Houston on the Galveston, Houston & Henderson, that was jointly owned by the I-GN and Katy. The GH&H Houston-Galveston line passed within sight of the BOQ barracks at Ellington Field, and it was populated mostly with Ten-Wheelers and Consolidations. There were three little MoPac passenger trains in each direction through Olcott that were Galveston connections for the *Texan*, *Southerner* and *Sunshine Special*.

The Laredo main line through San Marcos, however, featured some of the biggest MoPac steam power used on the Texas lines. The most notable of these were the handsome I-GN P-73 Pacifics 1151-1155 and StLB&M 1156-1161, and the heavy StLB&M MK-63 2-8-2s 1111-1120.

The locomotives on the Texas lines were at once typical and unique. They were standard MoPac designs but varied in details and were "rare"

OPPOSITE and BELOW / EMERY GULASH / MORNING SUN BOOKS COLLECTION

EMERY GULASH posed in his Civil Air Patrol uniform (above) in the early 1940s. St. Louis, Brownsville & Mexico 4-6-2 1157 (left) was at Houston's Belt Line Junction on the *Sunshine Special* in December 1945.

considering their isolated geographical working region.

Emery's excellent photo skills and good camera equipment captured an unexpected segment of the Missouri Pacific in its final decade of steam.

Texas Pacifics

BEFORE THEY WERE ACQUIRED by the Missouri Pacific in 1925, the International-Great Northern and St. Louis, Brownsville & Mexico had no large or modern power, and even their heavyweight *Sunshine Special* was dispatched behind 4-6-0s. To cure this problem, in 1927 they took delivery of five heavy Alco 4-6-2s based on the MoPac 6611-6629 class and assigned the new 1151-1155 to the International-Great Northern. These big Pacifics went right to work in Texas and stayed there for their entire careers. They were equipped with Baker valve gear, American front-end throttles. The cast Commonwealth pilot was applied to the 1153 in later years. In June 1945 the 1153 was fresh out of overhaul at the Kingsville Shop and was making a break-in run (right) on a 35-car freight at San Marcos before being returned to passenger duties. It showed up in September 1945 (opposite bottom) departing San Marcos with the southbound Laredo section of the *Sunshine Special*. Compare the details of the 1153 with sister 1154 (below) on *Sunshine Special* 1-21 at San Marcos in August 1945. A careful look will reveal she's "packin' the Irish," carrying green flags up by the stack to indicate a second section following. Before the postwar Eagle streamliners, the heavyweight *Sunshine Special* had sections out of St. Louis to Mexico City via Laredo, as well as to Los Angeles via El Paso and to Houston and Galveston.

THREE PHOTOS / EMERY GULASH / MORNING SUN BOOKS COLLECTION

FOUR PHOTOS / EMERY GULASH / MORNING SUN BOOKS COLLECTION

THE FIVE I-GN HEAVY PACIFICS of October 1926 were followed in June 1927 by six similar but slightly larger 4-6-2s for the St. Louis, Brownsville & Mexico. The 1156-1161, however, took a long time to get to home rails, as they were grabbed at St. Louis and pressed into service on the Missouri River line to Kansas City and Omaha where the Wabash and CB&Q were heating up the competition. The Brownsville Pacifics didn't get to Texas until the new *Eagle* streamliner took over on the Missouri line in 1940. The new Pacifics had Walschaertz valve gear and carried their air pumps behind pilot deck shields. Compare Brownsville Pacific 1156, on the southbound *Sunshine Special* at San Marcos in August 1945 (opposite top). I-GN 1155 was on the northbound *Special* there (below) a month later. The Brownsville 1157 (opposite bottom) was on a southbound troop train at San Marcos in July 1945, while the 1158 (above) showed off its Worthington feedwater pump at Houston in December 1947. Sharing the main line through San Marcos was the MKT, where Pacific 395 (opposite center) was on the *Texas Special* in July 1945.

BROWNSVILLE PACIFIC 1158 (opposite top) **was popping off and being blown down as it departed San Marcos on the** *Sunshine Special* **in August 1945, while 1160 was double-headed with 1156** (above) **there in the same month. The 1161 had less pleasant weather** (left) **in September 1945. A northern visitor, MoPac 6624,** (opposite bottom) **was at Belt Junction in Houston in December 1945 with No.25, the** *Texan*. **The I-GN P-73s were based on these engines but had Worthington instead of Elesco feedwater heaters applied.**

FOUR PHOTOS / EMERY GULASH / MORNING SUN BOOKS COLLECTION

IT IS IRONIC that in November 1926 Missouri Pacific President Lewis W. Baldwin turned to Alco to supply modern power for the recently acquired Texas lines. Ten heavy Mikados were built by Alco-Brooks for the St. Louis, Brownsville & Mexico that were based on the MoPac 1536-series. The engines were unusual in two ways. The 1111-1118 built were as oil burners, while 1119 and 1120 were equipped to burn low-grade lignite coal. Coal burning was less than satisfactory, and the dynamic duo was soon converted to oil, as well, but they remained distinctive in appearance with their two shielded cross-compound air pumps dominating the pilot decks. With no need for stokers, the oil burners were built with their air pumps mounted on the frame behind the firebox, hidden beneath the cab. Though this was a particularly inconvenient and dirty placement (and the only U.S. engines so equipped), the 1111-1118 kept their uniquely placed pumps throughout their careers, as evident on the 1116 (*opposite top*) at San Marcos in April 1945. Compare the front end with the 1119 (*above*), that was venting its Worthington feedwater heater as it departed San Marcos a month later. The ten StLB&M engines and MoPac 1536-1570 Mikados were unusual in a second aspect in that they had a space between their second and third drivers. When they were being built, the MP was experimenting with an identical engine, 1699, that was equipped with a third cylinder in the center that drove on the third axle, and provisions were incorporated in the MoPac and StLB&M engines for possible future conversion to three cylinders. Preceding the big Mikes on the Texas lines were ten copies of USRA Light Mikados. The I-GN Baldwins 1101-1110 were slightly lighter than the USRA originals. The 1109 (*opposite bottom*) was at San Marcos in April 1945.

Brownsville Mikes

THREE PHOTOS / EMERY GULASH / MORNING SUN BOOKS COLLECTION

ABOVE and BELOW / R. FILLMAN

ABOVE and BOTTOM / EMERY GULASH / MORNING SUN BOOKS COLLECTION

MISSOURI PACIFIC PUBLIC TIMETABLE / APRIL 1, 1965

CONVERTED LIGNITE-BURNER 1119 was at the San Marcos water tank (*above*) in May 1945 and San Antonio (*opposite bottom*) in July 1948. Note the cut-away smokebox front to clear the pumps and the gap between the second and third drivers for the third-cylinder conversion that was never applied. The 1118, in passenger service at San Antonio (*opposite top*) in December 1947, had its pumps moved from beneath its cab to the pilot deck like the 1119. The 1120 was scampering southward (*below*) out of San Marcos in September 1945. The StLB&M (*left*) ran between Houston and Brownsville, while the I-GN mains were Longview-Laredo and Ft. Worth-Houston.

FOUR PHOTOS / EMERY GULASH / MORNING SUN BOOKS COLLECTION

MISSOURI PACIFIC HEAVY MIKADO 1555 was easing a northbound freight (opposite top) out of the passing track at San Marcos in August 1945 after the *Sunshine Special* pulled in for its station stop. Well-maintained Missouri-Kansas-Texas 4-6-2 401 (below) had No.1, the southbound *Texas Special*, at MKT Junction in San Marcos in July 1945 passing a Missouri Pacific billboard in the distance. International-Great Northern 2-8-4 1122 was northbound at Belt Junction Tower 80 on the north side of Houston on Christmas day 1945 as the head brakeman (above) and conductor (opposite bottom) caught their orders from the operator at the joint FW&D-Rock Island main line diamond.

The SUNSHINE SPECIAL

This famous train, a travel favorite since 1915, will continue to provide daily through service between St. Louis-Memphis and El Dorado, Ark., Shreveport and Lake Charles, La., Houston, Austin, San Antonio and Mexico City.

MISSOURI PACIFIC PUBLIC TIMETABLE / MAY 30, 1948

THE *SUNSHINE SPECIAL* took on many different appearances, depending on where you saw it. International-Great Northern 4-6-0 342 (above) was hustling the Galveston section of No. 1-21 through League City, Texas, on the Galveston, Houston & Henderson in February 1946. The GH&H was right outside the window (below) of the bachelor officers' quarters at Ellington Field, where 2-22 was photographed in December 1946. The May 30, 1948, public timetable (left) reassured travelers that the reliable favorite *Sunshine Special* had not yet been replaced by the new *Texas Eagle* streamliners.

ABOVE and BELOW / EMERY GULASH / MORNING SUN BOOKS COLLECTION

Texas Ten-Wheelers

BELOW and BOTTOM / R. FILLMAN

INTERNATIONAL-GREAT NORTHERN Ten-Wheeler 378 (above) was romping toward Galveston with the *Sunshine Special* on July 19, 1948. Before the Pacifics arrived in the mid-1920s, these were the typical passenger engines on the Texas lines. The same engine was departing Houston Union Station (below) with the *Sunshine Special* on a different day in that same month.

THE TEXAS SUBSIDIARIES that were brought into the Missouri Pacific during the 1920s considered Ten-Wheelers and Consolidations to be "big" road power, with 2-6-0s and 4-4-0s filling in on lesser duties. These 4-6-0s and 2-8-0s were well suited to the region's gently rolling terrain, and many survived to the end of steam, often after modernization and rebuilding. The 378 (top and above) was part of the 371-384 series built in 1911 by Baldwin for the I&GN with Stephenson valve gear and slide valves.

THE MOST NUMEROUS of the Texas Ten-Wheelers were the 63-inch-drivered I-GN 315-360. In May 1945 the 328 (above) was working the Austin-San Antonio local at San Marcos, and it was there again (below) in August 1945. The footboards are a strong indication that this one was considered a freight engine, while sister 342 (page 20) had a traditional cowcatcher and was rebuilt for passenger service by having its drivers increased from 63 to 67 inches by applying thicker driver tires and getting Walschaertz valve gear.

TEN-WHEELER 383 was kicking up the dust at the San Marcos depot (above) in March 1945 with a northbound troop train headed for Fort Hood at Killeen. A wooden caboose brought up the markers (left) on the troop train. Another variation on the 315-360 series was the 350, that was working the local (below) at San Marcos in October 1945. This little freight engine kept its 63-inch drivers and footboards but was equipped with Walschaertz valve gear. The Ten-Wheelers had been built with high headlights.

R. FILLMAN

 # Miscellaneous Power

THE StLB&M HEAVY MIKADOS were based on the MoPac 1536-1570 series, and the 1544 of that class (above) was at Houston in December 1947. The gap between the second and third drivers is evident on the 1559 (below), at Dupo, Illinois, on March 28, 1953. An array of Mikados and Consolidation 32 (opposite lower center) were in the "winter garden" tracks at Dupo in September 1953. The 1480 (opposite bottom), at North Little Rock, Ark., on September 3, 1953, was typical of the MoPac's heavy Mikados 1401-1535. Consolidation 70 was clipping through the weeds (opposite top) at Tallulah, La., on June 19, 1953. The 1061 (opposite upper center), one of the C-57 2-8-0s on the GH&H, was nearing Galveston on July 18, 1948.

DON BALL COLLECTION

DON BALL COLLECTION

R. FILLMAN

T.J. McNAMARA

RAY LOWRY / LOU SCHMITZ COLLECTION

Switching with Steam

THREE PHOTOS / R. FILLMAN

WHEN THE 'MODERN" MoPac was created in 1924, it inherited a bewildering array of six-wheel switchers from the predecessor roads. Typical of the old-timers was the 9447 (right) from the group of 75 Class SW6-51s built in 1905-'06. It was working in Houston in July 1948. Much more orderly were the 85 USRA copy 0-8-0s. The first SW8-51s, 9701-9720, were built by Baldwin in 1924-'25. The 9706 is shown (opposite top) retired at North Little Rock on September 3, 1953. The 9725-9785 came from Lima and Alco with American front-end throttles, which pushed the headlights forward. The similar 9601-9605 were built by Alco for the StLB&M, while oil-burners 9606-9610 went to the I-GN. The 9606 (top) and 9610 (above) were at Palestine, Texas, in December 1947 and July 1948.

RAY LOWRY / LOU SCHMITZ COLLECTION

The End of Steam

MAC OWEN COLLECTION

EVEN THE MIGHTIEST must fall, and the Missouri Pacific managed to retire the last of its steam locomotives by 1956. The mightiest of the Missouri Pacific were the 15 heavy 4-8-4s (2201-2215) built by Baldwin in 1943. Due to wartime restrictions, these 73-inch-drivered machines were based on the D&RGW M68 4-8-4s of 1937. The 2203 (above) was at North Little Rock on September 3, 1953. In 1930 the MP had acquired 25 powerful but slow 63-inch-drivered 2-8-4s from Lima (1901-1925), and between 1940 and 1942 they were rebuilt by the Sedalia Shop with lengthened boilers and cast underframes into fast 75-inch-drivered 4-8-4s (2101-2125).

27

DONALD G. HILLS

Diesels and *Eagles*

CHAPTER TWO

THE MISSOURI PACIFIC was early to embrace internal combustion power, operating a respectable fleet of gas-electric motor cars dating as far back as 1906, with most of the fleet filling out between 1911 and 1931 with cars from General Electric, J.G. Brill and the Electro-Motive Company. In 1931 the subsidiary New Orleans & Lower Coast bought a Plymouth 30-ton four-wheel gas-mechanical that remained in service until October 1964!

The first diesel-electric locomotives purchased by the Missouri Pacific were two NC2 switchers (4100-4101) from the Electro-Motive Corporation in July 1937, along with four SC's. The long-framed NC's, powered by a 900-h.p. Winton 201A 12-cylinder engine, were the only ones of their type ever built. The SC's had a 600-h.p. 201A. The MoPac and its subsidiaries continued to purchase diesel switchers from EMC, Alco and Baldwin into the 1940s and beyond.

The Missouri Pacific really made diesel headlines, however, on March 10, 1940, when it introduced its two six-car *Eagle* trainsets, each powered by an EMC 2000-h.p. E3 "streamliner" cab unit. The E3 carried two 1000-h.p. V-12 versions of the new General Motors 567 two-cycle engine. The entire train was styled by industrial designer Raymond Loewy.

The new *Eagles* operated daily in each direction on a roughly ten-hour 478-mile schedule in direct competition with the steam-powered Wabash and Missouri-Kansas-Texas. The six-car trains were such a success, that an entire fleet of new *Eagles* replaced the steam-powered heavyweights as quickly as possible following the Second World War.

EMERY GULASH / MORNING SUN BOOKS COLLECTION

ELECTRO-MOTIVE E6s were featured (above) in MoPac advertising art for many years. Postwar E7 7016 (left) was heading up the *Colorado Eagle* at Denver on May 26, 1950, carrying the Loewy image of the original *Eagle*.

The War Production Board allocated a dozen A-B sets of EMC's new FT freight unit to the MoPac during the war, and internal combustion began to invade steam's ultimate stronghold, road freight service. With the arrival of the FT's, steam's fate was inevitable.

Hatching an *Eagle*

STEAM AND DIESEL shared the cover (below) on the December 15, 1940, pubic timetable with an eagle wings motif. Inside were ads for the streamliner that had been introduced on March 10, 1940, but the back cover still carried a full page ad for the *Sunshine Special* showing the interior of a heavyweight lounge car. At that time, the *Eagle*, between St. Louis and Omaha, was the Missouri Pacific's only streamliner.

MORNING SUN BOOKS COLLECTION

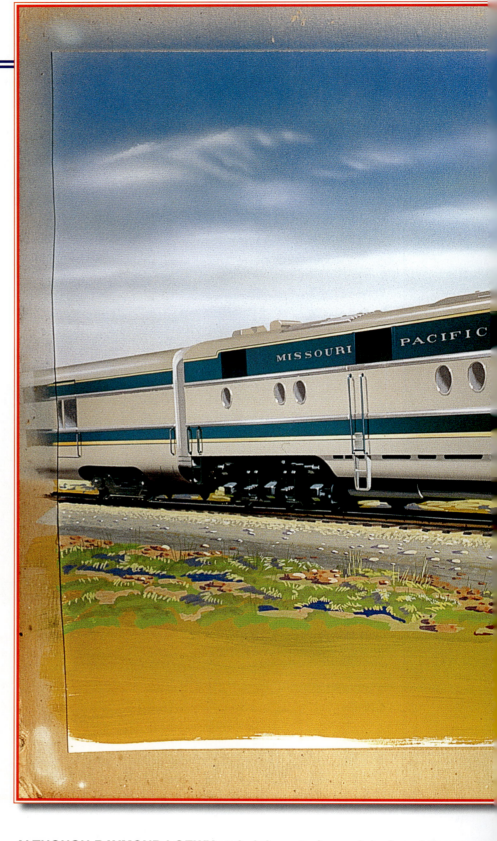

ALTHOUGH RAYMOND LOEWY styled the exterior and designed the interior of the *Eagle*, the slant-nose E3 was a standard Electro-Motive design in October 1939 when construction began on MoPac 7000-7001. It was the General Motors Styling Section in Detroit that applied Loewy's design to the locomotive. This original rendering shows that the GM artist, likely Leland Knickerbocker or Paul Meyer,

used an 11"x14" black and white photo as the underlying base for his "finished artwork." Removing the surrounding matte reveals the airbrush overspray that is a fascinating study in the artist's technique. An obviously Loewy touch in the physical carbody is the change from the EMC-standard rectangular side windows to portholes. Interestingly, Loewy seems to have adopted the distinctive curved side panel shape from the GM-designed Rock Island *Rocket* livery used on the TA units in 1937. It is likely that Loewy worked closely with the GM stylists. EMC became Electro-Motive Division of GM in January 1941.

THIS DRAMATIC EAGLE MURAL (above) decorated the curved back wall of the bar in the diner-lounge. Each of the two *Eagle* trainsets, built by American Car & Foundry, was comprised of a Railway Post Office baggage car, a mail storage car, two coaches, a diner-bar-lounge and a parlor observation car with a private drawing room. Being day trains, there were no sleeping accommodations, and the entire consist could accommodate only 170 passengers. The cars were made of aluminum alloy, and since ACF did not yet have Budd's shotwelding technology, they had to be riveted together. Loewy hated rivets and added an aluminum cap strip over the rivet panels that was continued right onto the locomotive, as well. The trainsets were gathered together in the winter of 1940 and taken out on the road for testing and publicity photos, which explains the snow cover and typically Missouri winter weather that made the pictures (opposite) somewhat less than was desired. Note on the original train that the "bow wave" from the pilot swept straight back to the cars, while on later units it was zigged down to the frame rivet strip just behind the cab steps and was also changed on the cars.

OFFICIAL GUIDE OF THE RAILWAYS / JULY 1940

Eastbound
No. 106-6—The Eagle
Streamlined Train
Reclining Coach—Omaha to St. Louis.
De Luxe Reclining Coach—Omaha to St. Louis.
Diner Bar Lounge—Omaha to St. Louis.
Parlor Observation Car—

The *Eagle* takes flight

TWO PHOTOS / AMERICAN CAR & FOUNDRY

MORNING SUN BOOKS COLLECTION

OFFICIAL GUIDE OF THE RAILWAYS / JULY 1940

MISSOURI PACIFIC LINES
CONDENSED SCHEDULES
ST. LOUIS AND THE WEST
ST. LOUIS–OMAHA–LINCOLN–MEMPHIS–NEW ORLEANS–KANSAS CITY–COLORADO–UTAH–CALIFORNIA.

R.L. SCHMIDT COLLECTION

JIM BOYD COLLECTION

MISSOURI PACIFIC PHOTO / JIM BOYD COLLECTION

THE NEW *EAGLE* streamliner was an immediate success. Its condensed schedule (opposite center) is shown as it appeared in the July 1940 *Official Guide of the Railways*. The image of the original *Eagle* (opposite top) was used on ticket forms long after the fleet expanded to the plural *"Eagles"* and the prototype train had become the *Missouri River Eagle*. The second streamliner in the fleet was to be the two-car *Dixie Eagle* between Memphis and Tallulah, La. (opposite Vicksburg, Miss.). The power was a unique "AA6" that was an EMC E6 with its rear engine removed and replaced with a baggage compartment. The 1000-h.p. 7100 was considered by EMC to be the last "motor car" it ever produced, though the MoPac always regarded it as a locomotive. The Memphis train was renamed the *Delta Eagle* before it went into service. The 7100 had been moved to the 208-mile Downs Branch in northern Missouri and was heading up No. 510-110-20 from Downs to Kansas City on March 10, 1956. In October 1941 the MoPac bought two cab-and-booster sets of EMD's now-standard 2000-h.p. E6 for the new *Colorado Eagle*. The 7002A/B and 7003A/B (above) differed visually from the E3s in having the downward zig in the frame stripe behind the cab and that the "Loewy curve" side panel was painted on instead of being an externally applied aluminum trim strip. Even though its number cannot be read from the distance, the unit in this publicity photo (above), taken along the Missouri River near Jefferson City, is one of the E6s.

35

IMMEDIATELY FOLLOWING the debut of the Eagle (below) on March 16, 1940, the MoPac began making plans to replace the *Scenic Limited* with a new *Colorado Eagle*. The two E6 sets were purchased for the Colorado service and construction began on the trainsets. With the onset of war after December 7, 1941, however, the new streamliner was almost stillborn. The government approved completion of the train to free up older equipment for the war emergency, and the *Colorado Eagle* made its debut with little fanfare on June 21, 1942. The MoPac line joined the D&RGW at Pueblo, where the *Eagle* turned north on the Joint Line to Denver, where it terminated. Connections were made at Pueblo with the Rio Grande's Royal Gorge route to the Western Pacific. Publicity artwork (above) featured 7003 and a wartime theme.

MISSOURI PACIFIC PHOTO / JIM BOYD COLLECTION

"Better trains follow General Motors Locomotives"

A roomy, sleep-inviting bedroom on a Missouri Pacific Eagle offers the comforts of a fine home, plus the ingenious planning of America's leading car builders.

GONE long ago are the "good old days" when no one really expected to get a good night's rest on a sleeping car — and privacy was at a premium. Gone too are the odors of oil lamps, the uncertain heat of wood-fired stoves, drafts, soot, cinders and the jerky sleep-destroying stops and starts so familiar to old-time travelers.

★ ★ ★

HERE now are such fast, crack trains as the *Missouri Pacific Eagles* with luxurious private sleeping quarters that invite restful, unbroken slumber. Then, to make assurance of smooth, clean, on-time riding, these trains are powered by General Motors Diesel locomotives on their long journeys between St. Louis and Denver, and throughout the Southwest.

Deep, refreshing sleep free from jolts and jars and noise, is just one more proof that better trains follow General Motors locomotives. A good thing to remember when you plan your next trip — anywhere.

ELECTRO-MOTIVE DIVISION OF GENERAL MOTORS
La Grange, Ill. • Home of the Diesel Locomotive

JOHN BRUNNER / LOU SCHMITZ COLLECTION

A. DEAN HALE

LOU SCHMITZ

Doodlebugs and the *Eaglet*

LINCOLN, NEBRASKA, was an important market for the MoPac, even though it was 47 miles west of the Missouri River main line between Kansas City and Omaha. To tap the state capital, the MoPac had a westward from the river line at Union, Nebraska. The connection from the main line trains to Lincoln had been handled for years with gas-electric motor cars like the 650, shown (left) at Lincoln on July 14, 1943, preparing to make the run to Union to connect with the *Eagle*. It was at Union (opposite center) on October 4, 1953. The 650 was a 1926 EMC 57-foot, 220-h.p. car with a St. Louis Car Company body. While a chugging doodlebug was appropriate to meet a heavyweight *Sunflower* or *Missourian*, the new streamlined *Eagle* was a different matter, so in March 1942 American Car & Foundry turned out a double-ended streamlined motor car similar to those built in 1940 for the New York, Susquehanna & Western. The new *"Eaglet"* was styled inside and out like Loewy's *Eagle*. It was powered by two Waukesha 210-h.p. diesels mounted under the floor and each driving a hydraulic torque converter to one of the trucks. The 670 covered two round trips a day to between Lincoln and Union to meet the *Missouri River Eagles*. It was Lincoln (bottom and opposite bottom) on November 26, 1953, and (below) on June 19, 1954. A short while later, the run was converted to a bus. The 670, repowered with 300-h.p. Cummins engines, was moved south to replace AA6 7100 (page 34) on the *Delta Eagle*. The 670 was finally retired and scrapped in 1960.

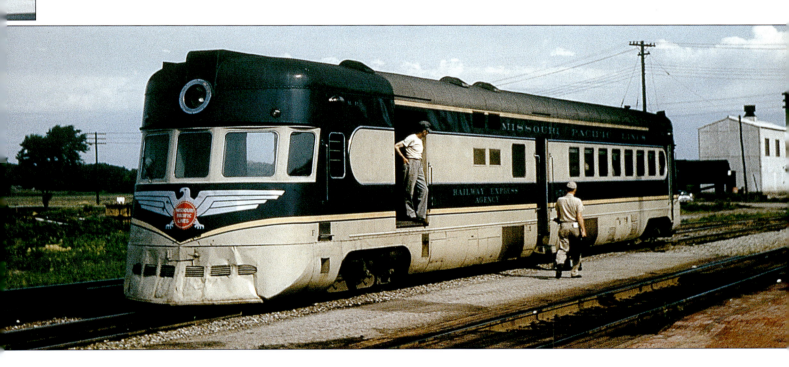

ABOVE and BELOW / LOU SCHMITZ

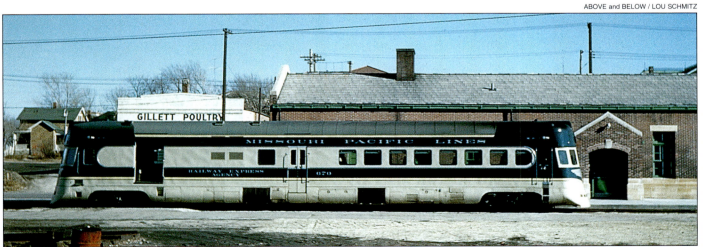

THREE PHOTOS / JIM NEUBAUER

The *Eagle* at Jefferson City

THE JOINT MISSOURI PACIFIC and Katy main line through Jefferson City, Missouri, follows the south bank of the Missouri River and passes right next to the state capitol building (page 71). In May 1954 Don Ball photographed No.6, the eastbound *Missouri River Eagle*, with E6 7002 (left) and a B-unit on the point and an original 1940 observation car (below) on the rear. The somewhat mixed consist and the Budd dome, one of three built for the *Colorado Eagle* in 1948, are evidence of the growth of this train. In July 1969, Chicagoan Jim Neubauer was riding one of the original *Eagle* obs cars on the westbound *Missouri River Eagle* No.5 (opposite) as it overtook a towboat on the river and then met a Katy freight at the Jefferson City passenger station. The *Eagle* was running "wrong main" to be on the station side for the meet. Note how relatively unchanged the station scene was from 1954 to 1969.

TWO PHOTOS / DON BALL

LOUIS A. MARRE

 ## More E's and More *Eagles*

R. FILLMAN

42

TWO PHOTOS / T.J. DONAHUE

AS SOON AS WARTIME restrictions were lifted, the MoPac went to EMD for more passenger units, and between September 1945 and June 1948 it acquired 14 E7 cab units (7004-7017) and eight boosters. The 7006 was leading a heavy *Missouri River Eagle* (above and right) out of St. Louis on a dreary day, while the road-weary 7011 (below) was bringing No.32, the *Sunshine Special*, in on September 12, 1960. The pristine I-GN 7007 (opposite bottom) was at Houston in July 1948, and the 7016 (opposite top) was looking almost as good at Little Rock on September 10, 1961.

AL HOLTZ

WALT GROSSELFINGER COLLECTION

A WHOLE NEW FLOCK of *Eagles* was introduced after the war. Two *Texas Eagles* out of St. Louis began on August 15, 1948, with the *West Texas Eagle* running El Paso and the *South Texas Eagle* to San Antonio and Houston. That same year the *Valley Eagle* was put on the StLB&M between Houston and Brownsville, and the *Louisiana Eagle* was introduced on the Texas & Pacific between New Orleans and Fort Worth. The schedules of all the *Eagles* south of St. Louis were coordinated for convenient connections. But not all trains were *Eagles*, however, as trains like the *Sunshine Special* and *Southerner* remained in the timetables. The 7014 (right) was at Texarkana with the *Southerner* in 1957 while its Texas sections were being shuffled. The 7004 (below) was at Little Rock on June 14, 1961, while the 7005 (above) was arriving in St. Louis in the early 1950s. The 7015 was leading a perfect A-B-A power set on a matched *Eagle* consist (opposite bottom) at what appears to be Kirkwood Hill in the 1950s. Interestingly, the MoPac E7s continued to be delivered with the Loewy portholes while nearly everyone else had E7s with rectangular windows. The EMD E8s, introduced in 1949, made portholes factory standard. The 7010 was arriving at Denver Union Station (overleaf) in June 1960 with the *Colorado Eagle* after an 18-hour, 1015-mile overnight trek from St, Louis.

LOUIS A. MARRE

DON BALL COLLECTION

WALT GROSSELFINGER COLLECTION

LOUIS A. MARRE

EMD's FT: Wartime Freight Diesels

AT THE BEGINNING of the Second World War in December 1941, the MoPac was already using E-units on the *Eagles* and a variety of diesel switchers in the yards. Knowing it would need more power, it put in a request for the only road freight units available at the time, the Electro-Motive 1350-h.p. FT, powered by the new 16-cylinder 567 two-stroke-cycle engine.

The War Production Board approved the MoPac's request in 1943, and four A-B sets were delivered in November and December that year. The 501-504 were drawbar-connected cab and booster sets. Four more A-B sets came in September and October 1944 (505-508), and they were followed by a final four (509-512) in July 1945. These eight sets were fitted with couplers on all units, and the boosters had hostler controls and a fifth porthole at the control stand. The FTs began the MoPac's long policy of no dynamic brakes. for hostling. The FT's began the MoPac's long policy of no dynamic brakes. The brand new 508 set (left), at Dupo, Ill., on October 27, 1944, clearly shows the top details, including the four flush cooling fans. The 509 (top) was the traiing unit at Van Buren, Ark., in September 1959. Note the hostler's porthole just ahead of the side door on the B-unit. The Electro-Motive Division full page color ad (opposite) from 1945 featured the MoPac's historic legacy and a pitch to "Buy <u>More</u> War Bonds."

LOUIS A. MARRE COLLECTION

48

It was a great day in railroading when in 1852 Missouri Pacific received its first locomotive delivered by sailing vessel and river boat from New England shops. This was the first locomotive to run west of the Mississippi.

Today Missouri Pacific uses a fleet of high powered General Motors Diesel locomotives to haul long heavy loads of oil and war freight, and to provide swift dependable passenger transportation.

PUTTING RAILROADING ON A NEW PLANE

THESE days the railroads are doing things that would have been impossible a few years ago. And one of their most powerful and modern tools is the General Motors line of Diesel locomotives.

Since the day that the first of these locomotives took the rails, they have rolled up the impressive total of more than 200 millions of miles of operation on America's major railroads.

In the things they have done—moving tremendous loads, maintaining fast, regular schedules, always on the job—lies the forecast of a new day for railroading when the war is over. Then the *full possibilities* in Diesel motive power may be applied to the carrying of passengers and freight throughout the country.

That is why it's a great new day for railroading, with greater days ahead.

ON TO FINAL VICTORY
BUY <u>MORE</u> WAR BONDS

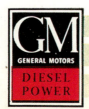

LOCOMOTIVES . . . . **ELECTRO-MOTIVE DIVISION**, La Grange, Ill.

ENGINES . . 150 to 2000 H.P. . . **CLEVELAND DIESEL ENGINE DIVISION**, Cleveland 11, Ohio

ENGINES . . . 15 to 250 H.P. . . . . . **DETROIT DIESEL ENGINE DIVISION**, Detroit 23, Mich.

The F3 Fleet

WARTIME EXPERIENCE with the FT's left the MoPac ready to dieselize as fast as possible when peace returned. EMD replaced its pioneering FT (after a total production of 555 cabs and 541 boosters) in July 1945 with the substantially improved 1500-h.p. F3. The MoPac began taking delivery in November 1947 with six A-B-A sets (513-524 and 513B-518B), along with two sets for the I-GN (525-528 and 525B-526B) and a dozen cab units for the StLB&M (529-540) These units were all classic "chicken wire" F3s, and none had dynamic brakes. The MoPac 520 (opposite top) was at St. Louis on April 12, 1961, while I-GN 526 (top left) was at Van Buren, Ark., on August 13, 1960. In June 1948 EMD delivered StlB&M cabs 541-552 and in August boiler-equipped MoPac A-B sets 561-566 and 561B-566B. The StLB&M 549 (above), at Houston in July 1948 with 535, shows the large side number boards and absence of chicken wire characteristic of the 1948 units. The final F3s were MoPac 571-576, also delivered in August 1948. The 574 was rolling through Arkansas (opposite bottom) in 1955 and at Van Buren (center) on September 8, 1961.

LOUIS A. MARRE

DON BALL COLLECTION

ABOVE and BELOW / A. DEAN HALE

LOUIS A. MARRE

IN 1941 ALCO was developing a lightweight 1500-h.p. engine one when the Second World War slowed the project but didn't kill it. In August 1945 Alco released its experimental Model 244 four-cycle turbocharged engine design for production at the McIntosh & Seymour plant in Auburn, N.Y. The GM&O had placed an order for 20 1500-h.p. freight units before the war, and on January 9, 1946, Alco began installing production V-12 244s into the new GM&O FA1s only 81 days after the completion of the first engine prototype. The 244 initially performed very well, and customers immediately lined up, including the MoPac, which ordered 20 FA1 cabs (301-320) and ten FB1 boosters (301B-310B), that were delivered in March and April 1948. The 303 was heading up a set of FA/FB1s and later FA/FB2s (right) at North Little Rock on September 10, 1961. The FA1s performed well enough that MoPac returned to Alco in 1950 for ten more FA1 cabs (321-330) and five FB1 boosters (321B-325B) that had been upped to 1600-h.p. The 324 cab and 324B were split by FB2 385B (top and above) at Texarkana in November 1961.

Covered Wagons from Schenectady

MISSOURI PACIFIC AD / JULY 1956 TRAINS MAGAZINE

LOUIS A. MARRE

A Handful of Hermaphrodites

THE FIRST TRUE ROAD SWITCHER was the Alco 1000-h.p. RS1 of 1940, powered by the massive 6-cylinder inline 539 engine. Alco and Baldwin both boosted that to 1500-h.p. in 1946. Although EMD actually had a 1000-h.p. road switcher in the NW5 of 1946, it began a project in 1947 to create a 1500-h.p. "Branch Line" unit. But instead of simply enlarging the NW5, EMD began with an F3 cab unit and tried to "carve" visibility into the external truss frame carbody. The result was the BL2, which was essentially an F3 with its sides pulled in to provide rearward and forward visibility. The BL2 had all the disadvantages of a cab unit combined with the worst features of a road switcher. It was accurately described as, "an F-unit with all the working space taken out." MoPac crews had a more descriptive term, "hermaphrodites." The MoPac took delivery of eight BL2s in the summer of 1948. EMD artwork (below), that was based on a Rock Island photo, as evidenced by the unique commuter cars, suggests that the MoPac considered using the BL2s as passenger engines. They were delivered, however, in freight livery with no steam generators.

EMD ARTWORK / JIM BOYD

BRAND NEW BL2 4104 was photographed (above) by the company photographer at North Little Rock in 1948, and 4107 (opposite top) was working its usual assignment at Hope, Ark., on September 5, 1959. The 4106 (top), at North Little Rock on December 31, 1961, would be traded to EMD before the next New Years Eve.

R.L. BORCHERDING / J.C. SEACREST COLLECTION

BOB'S PHOTOS

The Unique F5s

BETWEEN AUGUST AND SEPTEMBER 1948 EMD began to apply the new D27 traction motors and stainless steel Farr-Air grilles over the radiator air intakes to its otherwise standard F3s. Thus the F3s delivered between September 1948 and February 1949 were unofficially dubbed "F5s" after the upgraded but very similar-looking F7 was introduced in October 1948. The MoPac got two deliveries of these F5s, with four A-B-A sets for the I-GN (553-560 and 553B-556B) and four boiler-equipped A-B sets for the MoPac (567-570 and 567B-570B). The last pair of that last set, 570/570B, was on the CB&Q delivery track (opposite center) off the Indiana Harbor Belt at Congress Park, Ill., just north of the EMD plant at La Grange, in September 1948. The 553 was leading a newer F7 (left) at North Little Rock on September 10, 1961. The 568 (below) was at St. Louis on April Fools Day 1961. And speaking of April Fools, earlier F3 547 (opposite bottom) was masquerading as an F5 with new grilles at the same spot on February 2, 1961.

LOUIS A. MARRE

MATT HERSON

RAILFAN & RAILROAD COLLECTION

58

Babyfaces

IN THE POSTWAR YEARS the locomotive builders could not keep up with the demand for diesels, and the only model with a proven track record was the Electro-Motive FT. The MoPac had been satisfied with its "baker's dozen" of VO switchers and had more newer switcher models on order, so in late 1948 it placed an order with Baldwin for four A-B sets of 1500-h.p. road freight units. Based on units previously delivered to the Jersey Central and New York Central, these "babyface" carbody DR4-4-1500s (201-208 and 201B-208B) carried steam generators and were three feet longer than the CNJ and NYC units. They had pneumatic controls and could not multiple with other models, so they always operated in "pure" sets. The 201 and 205 (left) were at Texarkana in 1957, while the 206 (opposite bottom) was captured by C.T. Wood at Sandy Hook, Mo., along the Missouri River. The same unit was on the point (below) at Barretts Station, Mo., in September 1953 (also see page 74).

R.S. PLUMMER / DON BALL COLLECTION

THOMAS J. McNAMARA

OOPS! StLB&M F7 616 got away from the hostler at Texarkana in 1953 (above) and rolled into the turntable pit. Faring much better were the MoPac 580 (right) at North Little Rock on July 10, 1961, and 621 (below) at Omaha on April 1, 1962. Note no dynamic brakes.

 ## More Power: F7s and E8s

IMMEDIATELY FOLLOWING the last "F5s" in September 1948, EMD continued MoPac deliveries with its new 1500-h.p. F7, MoPac 577-594, I-GN 595-606 and StLB&M 607-614, plus boosters MP 587B-594B and I-GN 595B-596B. Deliveries resumed in April 1950 and March 1951 on St.LB&M 615-616, I-GN 617-618 and MP 619-626, along with F7B's 619B-620B. StlB&M 611-614 and I-GN 617-618 were equipped with steam boilers.

SHARING THE ELECTRICAL and mechanical upgrades of the F7s were the new 2250-h.p. passenger E8s, powered by two V12 567B engines in a completely new internal carbody configuration and new radiator systems compared to the E3s, E6s and E7s. In June 1950 the MoPac acquired four E8s (7018-7021). The 7020 and a mate (above) were backing the *Colorado Eagle* into St. Louis Union Station in August 1950.

WITH A 22-UNIT FLEET of EMD E7 cabs and boosters and seven prewar slant-noses on hand by mid-1948, the MoPac still had a lot of passenger trains rolling behind big Pacifics. The railroad was not unfamiliar with Alco's big 2000-h.p. PA1, that had been introduced in mid-1946, as the *Eagle* pulled alongside Santa Fe's in Kansas City and those of the Katy, Pennsy and Wabash in St. Louis, as well as the SP's Texas & New Orleans fleet in Texas. In 1949 the MoPac placed an order for eight Spec DL304B PA1s (8001-1008), that were delivered in October and November. Impressed with the big units, the MoPac ordered four more (MP 8009-8010 and I-GN 8011-8012) that in May 1950 were the first Spec DL304C 2250-h.p. PA2s delivered to a customer. Six more (8013- 8018) were delivered in May and June 1951. At 7:50 in the morning on September 12, 1960, PA1 8002 at St. Louis Union Station (opposite top) with commuter No.36, known as the "*Kirkwood Eagle*" (though it actually came in from Pacific, Mo.) and backed out (opposite) a short while later. Shortly after that, PA2 8016 (below) arrived with No.10, the *Missourian* from Kansas City.

THREE PHOTOS / AL HOLTZ

Alcos for the *Eagles*

MAC OWEN COLLECTION

AL HOLTZ

CONTINUING WITH AL HOLTZ' morning in the St. Louis Union Station terminal tower (pages 58-59) on September 12, 1960, No.22, the *Texas Eagle* (above) from Mexico City and Laredo, arrived at 8:25 a.m. behind PA2 8020. Often erroneously referred to as "PA3s" because of the styling change that eliminated the curved "drip strip" trim behind the cab, the 8019-8036, delivered in the summer of 1952, were actually DL304C PA2s. Two days before his Monday morning in the tower, Al Holtz caught No.4, the *Ozarker* (opposite center) arriving in St. Louis with PA's and pulling alongside the departing L&N Nos. 93-81 to Nashville, the *Humming Bird* to New Orleans and *Georgian* to Atlanta. After clearing the east end of the wye (opposite bottom), the *Ozarker* would back into the stub terminal. Note the coaches-only consist on the overnight *Ozarker* from Ft. Worth. The 8035 (opposite top) was making a westbound station stop at Kirkwood in May 1961. There was an E8 and PA (top) on the *Missouri River Eagle* in Missouri in 1956.

GAYLORD PLUMMER / DR. ART PETERSON COLLECTION

ABOVE and BELOW / AL HOLTZ

THE FIRST "REAL" DIESELS on the MoPac were six EMC switchers acquired in July 1937 powered by Winton 201A engines. The 9000-9003 were 600-h.p. Model SC (Six hundred h.p. with Cast frames) with 8-cylinder inline engines, while 4100-4101 were 900-h.p. NC2 (Nine hundred h.p. with Cast frame) with V-12 engines. SC 9001 was sold in December 1959 to the short line Dardenelle & Russellville as No.14. It had changed little except in paint job (opposite bottom) at Russellville, Ark., in an evening twilight in November 1969. The next units were two Model SW (600-h.p. Welded frame) for the Union Terminal Railway of St. Joseph as 5 and 10 in May and December 1938, respectively. They were later transferred to the St. Joseph Belt, where the 10 (above) was still at work on February 5, 1958. In 1939 EMC introduced its 600-h.p. SW1, with a V-6 version of its new 567 engine. Between January 1939 and June 1941 the MoPac and its subsidiaries picked up eleven SW1s and added one more, St. Joseph Belt 12, in April 1947. The system's tenth SW1, MP 9006, was working the Ft. Smith Suburban Railway (below) on July 6, 1961.

LOUIS A. MARRE

Black Switchers

EMC 1939 ADVERTISEMENT

TWO OF THE MOST INTERESTING of the MoPac's early switchers were EMC demonstrators 823 and 824 (also their builders numbers), built in August 1938. The only NW4s ever produced, each of these 900-h.p. units, powered by a V-12 Winton 201A, carried a steam generator and rode on the trucks salvaged from the historic EMC boxcab passenger unit prototypes 511 and 512, built in 1935, that evolved into the E-units. The EMC 824 (above) became MoPac 4103 and worked until 1961!

LOU SCHMITZ

JIM BOYD

LOUIS A. MARRE

R.H. CARLSON

THE NEW ORLEANS & LOWER COAST bought the MoPac Lines' first internal-combustion locomotive in 1931: a second hand 63-ton Plymouth gas-mechanical. By 1935 it had three more, and the NO&LC 3002 was nearly identical to the Lee County Central engine (opposite bottom left), shown at Lee Center, Ill., in March 1970. In October 1940 the MoPac got Davenport-Bessler 803 (opposite bottom right), the first of 16 center-cab 44-tonners from D-B, Whitcomb, Porter and General Electric between then and January 1942. The 44-ton weight permitted the railroad to run them without a fireman, and the MoPac used them for light yard work at outlying facilities. GE tonners 800 and 811 (opposite center) were on their regular assignment at Springfield, Mo., in April 1954. StLB&M Baldwin VO1000 9154 (above), at Harlingen, Texas, on March 24, 1945, was one of six delivered to the Texas lines in February and March 1941. By mid-1946 the system had 14 VO1000s.

DON BALL COLLECTION

AFTER THE WAR the MoPac rapidly expanded its diesel switcher fleet. Baldwin 9120 (opposite bottom), on January 9, 1954, was one of 25 DS4-4-1000(SC)s acquired in 1948 and 1949. The 9177 (above), at Omaha on August 20, 1961, was one of 42 1200-h.p. EMD SW9s built in 1951 and 1952. Baldwins 9226 and 9223 (opposite top), at North Little Rock on September 10, 1961, were two of 40 1200-h.p. S12s built in 1951-'52.

ABOVE and BELOW / DON BALL COLLECTION

AMERICAN LOCOMOTIVE COMPANY / BOB'S PHOTOS

Geeps

THE FIRST ROAD SWITCHERS on the MoPac were four 1500-h.p. Alco RS2s. The TP-MP Terminal of New Orleans got 21 and 22 in April 1948, while the Texas & Pacific 1100, built January 1949, became TPMPT 23. The fourth and final RS2 was Missouri-Illinois 61, that posed (above) in lousy weather for its builders photo in November 1949. The next road switchers were four Baldwin DRS4-4-1500s, built for the StLB&M (4112-4115) in February 1949. That year EMD brought back semi-retired engineer Dick Dilworth to design a true road switcher to replace the unwieldy BL2. His result was the classic high-nose GP7 that put the 1500-h.p. power package of an F7 onto a girder frame with an offset cab like the Alco RS1 and RS2 and Baldwin road switchers. The MoPac bought the first of 208 GP7s in July 1950.

WALT GROSSELFINGER COLLECTION

MISSOURI PACIFIC LINES GP7s were numbered 4116-4194 and 4197-4325, assigned to MP, I-GN and StLB&M (see roster on page 124). The 4142-4149 and 4241-4260 were equipped with steam generators, and the 4157 (above) was in passenger service at Houston in February 1968. A pair of passenger Geeps (opposite bottom) on Newport-Kansas City Trains 210 and 211 were meeting near Yellville on the White River Line on October 29, 1959. Freight Geep 4184 (top), built in May 1950, was at Topeka, Kansas, in December 1959.

LOU SCHMITZ

NINETEEN OF THE FA2s, 361-373 and 387-392, were equipped with steam boilers for passenger service and are often considered "FPA2s." The 368 (below) was westbound at Texarkana in May 1957. The 376 (above) was heading up a set at the Omaha engine terminal on August 7, 1960. With the Missouri State Capitol building majestic in the background, FA2s 350 and 383 (right) were idling alongside the main line at Jefferson City in May 1954.

LOUIS A. MARRE

A. DEAN HALE

Alco FA2s

MANAGEMENT MUST HAVE BEEN HAPPY with the 45 FA1s and FB1s of 1948 and 1950 (page 52), because in the spring of 1951 it returned to Alco for the first of 102 1600-h.p. FA2s and FB2s. The numbering of the cab units began at 331, following FA1 330. The FA2 carbody was designed from the onset to accommodate a steam boiler and was two feet longer than the FA1. The most notable difference was the FA2 radiator grille moved forward, away from the end of the unit. Compare FB2 385B (above), at Texarkana in November 1961, with the FA1 and FB1 coupled to it.

DON BALL COLLECTION

JIM BOYD COLLECTION

THREE PHOTOS / THOMAS J. McNAMARA

MISSOURI PACIFIC PUBLIC TIMETABLE / MARCH 18, 1951

MORE POWER

When and Where it's needed

ONE OF the earliest and now one of the most extensive users of diesel locomotives, MISSOURI PACIFIC continues to expand its impressive array of this modern railroad motive power.

Locomotive shops are constructing for the MISSOURI PACIFIC system 124 additional new diesel units. When all have been placed in service this summer MISSOURI PACIFIC's principal passenger trains and most of its through freight trains will be diesel-powered. More than 66 per cent of the through freight tonnage will move behind diesel power.

Swift, rugged and flexible, with long-sustained availability for service, MISSOURI PACIFIC's growing diesel fleet provides the power needed now to assure dependable transportation for a re-arming nation and for business and industry in the West-Southwest Empire served by MISSOURI PACIFIC Lines.

SERVING THE WEST-SOUTHWEST EMPIRE

THE BACK COVER of the March 18, 1951, MoPac public timetable (right) featured a politically correct mix of EMDs and Alcos as it promoted the purchase of "124 additional new diesel units" for 1951 delivery. The units referenced included 45 GP7s, 19 FA2s, ten F7s and more than 40 EMD and Baldwin switchers. The 392, the last of the passenger equipped FPA2s, was leading a freight set (above left) at an unidentified location. The sequence of the FA2s at Barretts Station, Mo., in September 1953 began with westbound 355 (opposite bottom) pulling up and stopping. A short while later, the 335 (opposite center) came grinding up Kirkwood Hill through the cut that bypassed the old west tunnel and met the 355 (below). The photographer was standing on the sidings for the new National Museum of Transportation site. Also see the Baldwins (page 59) that passed shortly thereafter.

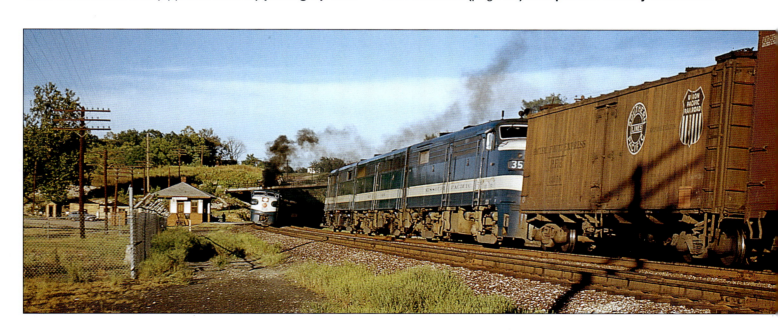

Baldwin AS16s and Alco RS3s

ST. LOUIS, BROWNSVILLE & MEXICO Baldwin AS16 4329 had been renumbered 938 by the time it was photographed (above) at Palestine, Texas, on July 23, 1963 (above). Less than a year later (below), on January 19, 1964, it was a bit the worse for wear at Houston and would survive only one more year.

LOUIS A. MARRE

IN APRIL 1948 the TP-MP Terminal of New Orleans bought two Alco RS2s (page 71), that were the MoPac Lines' first road switchers. The St. Louis, Brownsville & Mexico picked up four Baldwin DS4-4-1500s (4112-4115) in February 1949, and the International-Great Northern turned to Eddystone in November 1951 for a pair of 1600-h.p. AS16s (4195-4196). In mid-1964 the StLB&M bought six AS16s (4326-4331), that became the MoPac Lines' last Baldwin road units. Meanwhile, the Missouri-Illinois (page 112) had followed up its lone RS2 (61) of November 1949 with a pair of RS3s in 1951, and by 1955 had amassed a fleet of 13 RS3s (62-74). In January 1955 the MoPac itself began taking delivery on 26 of the 1600-h.p. RS3s (4501-4526), powered by turbocharged 12-cylinder 244 engines. The 4521 (right) was parked in the mid-day shade at Fort Scott, Kansas, in August 1958. Note it is set up for short-hood-forward operation. The 4511 and 4510 (above) were at North Little Rock on July 10, 1961. When they were new, the 244-powered Alcos (FA's and RS2s and RS3s) were rugged and reliable units, but as they got older, the inherent flaws in the 244 engine design began to affect their reliability and maintenance costs, and the road switchers were soon relegated to yard duty.

EMERY GULASH / MORNING SUN BOOKS COLLECTION

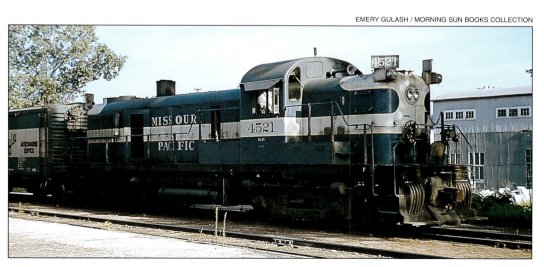

77

LOUIS A. MARRE

LOUIS A. MARRE

The Last of the First Generation

BY THE SUMMER OF 1955 the MoPac Lines rostered 218 GP7s, and the last steam engines were dead. Following the final GP7 (I-GN 4325) in May 1954, the MoPac began taking delivery in January 1955 on 40 of EMD's new 1750-h.p. GP9s (4332-4371). After the arrival of the 4371 in April 1955, the MoPac got no more new diesels until October 1959, when it gave Alco an order for a dozen 1800-h.p. RS11s (4601-4612) powered by the new 12-cylinder 251 engine. The RS11s rode on the trucks from retired Baldwin DR4-4-1500 Babyface units and retained their big Westinghouse traction motors. Like the Geeps and RS3s, the RS11s were set up for short-hood-forward operation. EMD matched Alco's 1800-h.p. rating with its upgraded GP18, and in the spring of 1960 the MoPac took delivery of 26 GP18s (4801-4826) with high short hoods.

LOUIS A. MARRE

EMD ARTWORK / FRONT COVER, JANUARY 10, 1955, *RAILWAY AGE*

MISSOURI PACIFIC'S "PLAIN VANILLA" GP9s with no dynamic brakes were featured in full color EMD advertising (above) in 1955. The real thing, 4345 (top), was heading up a set of newer GP18s through Van Buren, Ark., in April 1962. GP18s 4802 and 4803 were at Van Buren (opposite top) on August 13, 1960. Three RS11s (opposite bottom) were at North Little Rock on July 10, 1961. Note how stripe differs from the Geeps.

Eagle Merchandise Service

IN THE DAYS BEFORE FedEx and United Parcel Service, the Railway Express Agency and the railroads themselves provided parcel services that were faster and more "trackable" than the U.S. Post Office. In the early 1950s the MoPac introduced its "*Eagle* Merchandise Service" to handle this potentially lucrative on-line business and rebuilt a fleet of 36-foot and 40-foot boxcars for the service and painted them in a colorful and distinctive livery. A full page timetable ad (opposite) in March 1951 described the MP and T&P service and its early "Speedbox" attempt at containerization. *Eagle* box 48073 (above) was spotted for loading at the Fort Scott, Kansas, depot in August 1958, while the 48324 (below) was in the consist of the local behind the RS3. The 46960 (opposite top) was at Omaha on January 30, 1954.

ABOVE and BELOW / EMERY GULASH / MORNING SUN BOOKS COLLECTION

LOU SCHMITZ

MISSOURI PACIFIC PUBLIC TIMETABLE / MARCH 15, 1951

"SPEEDBOXES"—For EAGLE MERCHANDISE SERVICE

Another Missouri Pacific "First"

AS A FURTHER convenience for its patrons and to implement the Eagle Merchandise service recently established for shippers of less-than-carload merchandise freight along the railroad, Missouri Pacific has devised the "Speedbox."

This innovation in freight-handling efficiency and economy is the result of two years of experiment by Missouri Pacific traffic and operating men. Briefly, the "Speedbox" is a mobile but sturdy metal container mounted on casters, easy to handle empty or loaded. Its purpose is to save time in the packing, handling and loading of merchandise and to provide a further protection against loss and damage.

In operation, an empty "Speedbox" is delivered to the shipper's warehouse by a Missouri Pacific pick-up and delivery truck. Mobility of the box permits the shipper to move it to any part of his warehouse, transferring merchandise from shelf or bin directly into the box. Special packing is unnecessary because of the sturdy construction of the mobile container.

When loaded, the box is sealed, moved to the freight station by a pick-up truck, loaded into a merchandise car. On arrival at its destination the loaded box is delivered to the consignee who may unload it at his convenience.

Currently, use of "Speedboxes" is limited between certain stations on the Missouri Pacific Lines. Eventually it is expected these efficient mobile containers will be available for system-wide use and ultimately for interline freight movement.

Any Missouri Pacific traffic representative will be glad to supply complete information about "Speedboxes" and EAGLE MERCHANDISE service.

Top view above shows a "Speedbox" being loaded in shipper's warehouse and in lower view the loaded box is being trucked into a merchandise car. Left, the distinctive blue and grey color scheme readily identifies the cars assigned exclusively to Missouri Pacific's new EAGLE MERCHANDISE service.

FOUR PHOTOS / AL HOLTZ

GRAND AVENUE TOWER M is where the Terminal Railroad Association of St. Louis trackage ends 1.8 miles west of Union Station and splits into the Wabash, the Frisco and the Missouri Pacific's line to Iron Mountain Junction, where it splits for the lines south to Little Rock and west to Kansas City. Al Holtz spent an afternoon overlooking the junction on Sunday, September 11, 1960. The first action was Alco S2 switcher 9113 (below), built in 1944, westbound with a transfer freight. The *Colorado Eagle*, No.11 (opposite lower), out of Union Station at 4:00 p.m., rolled westward behind A-B E7s and a PA. The *Eagle* was followed by a freight (left) powered by F-units bracketing a pair of Geeps. Al's action concluded with No.4, the *Ozarker* (opposite bottom inset) from Ft. Worth, Texas, on time for its 4:40 p.m. arrival at Union Station. The dome was not an advertised feature of this all-stop workhorse train.

Grand Avenue Junction: September 11, 1960

The Texas & Pacific

CHAPTER THREE

IN THE "ERA OF THE *EAGLES*" the Texas & Pacific was an integral part of the Missouri Pacific system operations. Because of its history and economics and the laws of the state Texas, however, it benefitted both railroads to keep the T&P a separate entity. In its headquarters in Dallas, the T&P maintained its own executive and operating departments.

Had it not been for the looming Civil War, the Texas Pacific could have been the first transcontinental railroad, with the shortest and easiest was completed on December 15, 1881, when the T&P linked up at Sierra Blanca with the eastward-reaching Southern Pacific. The T&P completed its modern route map in 1882 when it built and bought a line eastward from Shreveport to New Orleans.

Like the MoPac, the T&P was in and out of bankruptcy in 1885 and 1916 and was often a pawn of the robber barons. During reorganization in 1923, the Missouri Pacific gained stock control of the T&P and secured the relationship over the next few

BELOW and LEFT / MARVIN H. COHEN

AL HOLTZ

RED DIAMONDS on MoPac colors characterized the T&P covered wagon fleet. The T&P adopted the *Eagle* livery for its eight E7s (2000-2007) of March 1947 and added the red diamond. The 2001 (bottom left) had the *West Texas Eagle* No.2 arriving at St. Louis on September 12, 1960. A pair of E7s (above) and a set of one-year-old F7s (top left) were at El Paso, Texas, in 1951.

route between an Atlantic seaport on the Gulf of Mexico and the Pacific Coast. Its route was surveyed by 1855, but construction did not begin until the 1870s between Shreveport, La., and Fort Worth. It also had a line to Texarkana and Sherman, Texas. Jay Gould gained control of the T&P in 1880 and began to lay track westward. The nation's second transcontinental years. It was a good investment, because the Texas oil boom put the T&P in the black from 1924 onward.

The T&P pursued its own motive power policy in the steam era and pretty much mimicked the MoPac in the diesel era, though from its red diamond herald to dynamic brakes and Swamp Holly Orange hood units, it displayed fascinating individuality.

85

ROBERT F. COLLINS

T&P PRESIDENT J.L. LANCASTER did not subscribe to MoPac President Baldwin's "black engine" mandate. In the 1940s T&P 4-6-2s and 4-8-2s were adorned in blue and gray, as shown on Pacific 711 (above) at Shreveport on May 22, 1949; passenger 4-8-2s were similarly adorned. The T&P's most famous steam locomotives were the prototype Lima 2-10-4s of 1925 that gave the "Texas" type its name. The T&P had 70 of the long-legged monsters. In 1976 the 610, by then the sole surviving T&P 2-10-4, displayed in Ft. Worth, was restored to service for the Texas leg of the *American Freedom Train*. In 1977 it was leased by the Southern Railway for excursion service and was steaming (below) in Cincinnati, Ohio, on July 17.

JIM BOYD

Steam on the Texas & Pacific

SWITCHER 466 was one of the 14 "government" USRA 0-6-0s (457-470) allocated to the T&P from Alco/Pittsburgh in 1919. It was working alongside Kansas City Southern E6 24 (above) at Texarkana in December 1947. The T&P was completely dieselized by April 1952, and its steam locomotives were soon scrapped. In May 1957, however, the T&P was obliged to lease 2-8-2 454 from the Ft. Worth & Denver (top) to pull trains over flooded main tracks at Bryce, La., where the diesels' traction motors dared not tread.

A. DEAN HALE

THE FIRST ROAD DIESELS on the Texas & Pacific were eight E7s that were delivered in March 1947 in the MoPac's Raymond Loewy *Eagle* livery. These were followed in 1949 by two more E7s and 16 A-B sets of F7s, that wore the GM-designed MoPac freight livery that had been introduced on the FT's in 1943. All switchers up to this time wore basic black. With the first seven GP7s (1110-1116) of March 1950, however, the T&P took off in a radical new direction with a Swamp Holly Orange carbody with black trim, rendered (below) by the EMD Styling Section. There was nothing like this on the MoPac!

A. DEAN HALE

EMD ARTWORK / EMERY GULASH / MORNING SUN BOOKS COLLECTION

88

Swamp Holly Orange

THE SWAMP HOLLY ORANGE was fresh (above) on GP7 1114 at Ft. Worth in August 1961. Sister 1116 (below) was a bit the worse for wear at the Ft. Worth passenger station in July 1959. The T&P filled out its high-nose Geep roster with 14 more GP7s (1117-1130) in 1951 and 1952 and 14 dynamic-brake-equipped GP9s (1131-1144) in the spring of 1957. In 1959 some Geeps were repainted into a blue and gray version of the orange scheme, as shown (opposite top) at Ft. Worth in October 1960. Note dynamic brakes on the F7s.

LOUIS A. MARRE

A. DEAN HALE

THE SWITCHER FLEET was also given the Swamp Holly Orange treatment, as shown (above) on SW7 1022 at Sweetwater, Texas, in July 1958 and on NW2 1006 (opposite bottom) at Dallas on September 12, 1960. Swamp Holly Orange was a rich orange when new but tended to lighten up a lot as it weathered. The T&P's first diesel was NW2 1000, built by EMD in November 1946. It was still in its basic black factory livery (opposite top) at Dallas in November 1950, before being repainted into the orange. In January 1949 the T&P bought a single Alco 1500-h.p. RS2. The 1100 was in the Marshall Shop (below) in the orange livery. It was the only non-EMD unit ever rostered by the T&P and was transferred to the TP-MP Terminal of New Orleans in the early 1950s as No. 23. After retiring in 1967, it became Alton & Southern 33.

BILL G. SHARP COLLECTION

CHARLES MIZELL, JR.

BOB'S PHOTOS

T&P Switchers – Orange and Otherwise

Variations on an *Eagle*

AL HOLTZ

WHILE THE MISSOURI PACIFIC got FT's and F3s between 1943 and 1948, the first freight covered wagons on the Texas & Pacific were 118 1500-h.p. F7s (83 cabs, 1500-1582, and 35 boosters, 1500B-1534B) delivered between February 1949 and August 1951. Unlike their MoPac brethren, the T&P F7s were all equipped with dynamic brakes for the West Texas hills and carried Mars signal lights in the nose housing and their headlight in the nose door. The 1547 (right) at Mineola, Texas, in 1957, presents the classic image of the T&P F7s. In 2004, MP Historical Society President Jim Ogden summed it up perfectly: "The T&P looked like a he-man version of the MoPac, with signal lights, dynamic brakes and a Texas-sized attitude." Following up on its eight 2000-h.p. E7s (2000-2007) of March 1947, the T&P added two more E7s (2008-2009) in April 1949 and then completed its passenger roster with eight 2250-h.p. E8s (2010-2017) in August 1951. E8 2012 (above) and an E7 were at St. Louis Union Station on September 12, 1960. The T&P never owned any PA's or other Alco passenger units.

DON BALL COLLECTION

LOUIS A. MARRE COLLECTION

E8 2013 WAS AT EL PASO (above) with No.7, the *Southerner*, on December 12, 1952. In addition to its E-units, the T&P had four boiler-equipped F7 cabs (1500-1501 and 1581-1582) and four boosters (1531B-1534B), all of which wore the *Eagle* passenger livery. The 1500 (opposite center left) was at Ft. Worth on February 12, 1961, and one of the boosters (opposite center right) was in freight service at Dallas the previous day. E8 2015 (opposite bottom) was teamed up with booster 1533B at Texarkana in the mid-1950s.

A. DEAN HALE

A. DEAN HALE

BILL G. SHARP

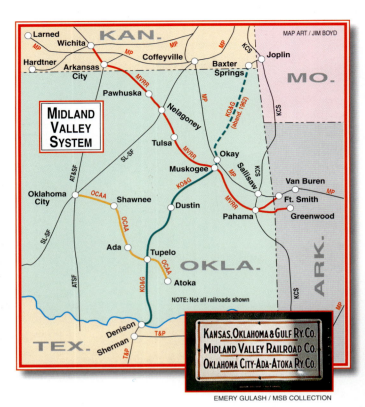

EMERY GULASH / MSB COLLECTION

 ## The Midland Valley

THE MUSKOGEE COMPANY acquired control of the Midland Valley; the Kansas, Oklahoma & Gulf and the Oklahoma City-Ada-Atoka Railway in 1930 and worked closely with the MoPac and Texas & Pacific as a western shortcut between Kansas and Texas. The Muskogee roads came under T&P control in 1964.

LOU SCHMITZ

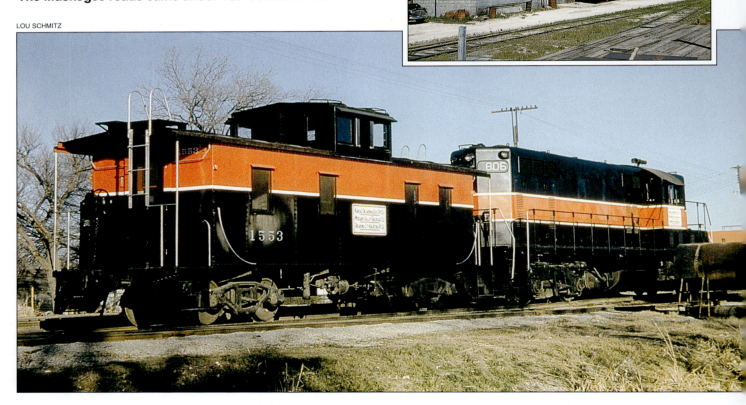

FIVE PHOTOS / EMERY GULASH / MORNING SUN BOOKS COLLECTION

KANSAS, OKLAHOMA & GULF got two A-B-A F7 sets in April 1949 in MoPac livery (right) for run-through service. When the KO&G and Midland Valley got GP7s (KO&G 801-809 and MV 151-154) in 1952-'53, however, they arrived in a unique black and orange livery. Midland Valley 154 (above) was at Wichita (opposite inset) in May 1960, while KO&G 806 (opposite bottom) was at Ada, Okla., on January 30, 1955. KO&G 809 was at an unidentified location (below) in 1960.

THE KO&G HAD A FLEET of distinctive rib-side hoppers with large side lettering to serve the coalfields around Fort Smith, Arkansas. There was one (below) in the distance behind Midland Valley 154 at Fort Smith on September 7, 1961, and being shoved by a 2-6-0 (above) in August 1960. The KO&G killed its USRA 2-8-2s and 2-10-2s with the delivery of the Geeps in the early 1950s, but steam continued to be used on the East Jordan & Southern in northwest lower Michigan, where the hopper was photographed.

LOUIS A. MARRE

FOUR PHOTOS / EMERY GULASH / MORNING SUN BOOKS COLLECTION

MIDLAND VALLEY GP7 154 was working (above) at Wichita in May 1960. On its train that day was caboose 1548 (right) that carried the "Sooner to and through the Southwest" herald (below). With their train together, the crew was preparing to depart Wichita (bottom) and run southeast toward Muskogee on the Midland Valley main.

EMERY GULASH / MORNING SUN BOOKS COLLECTION

BELOW and BOTTOM / LOUIS A. MARRE

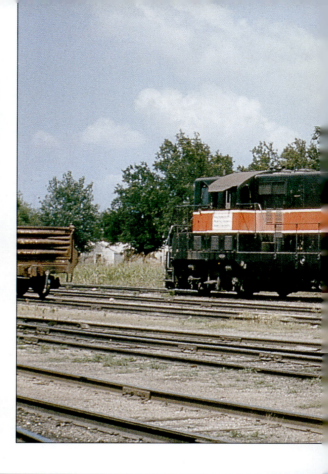

98

ABOVE and BELOW / LOUIS A. MARRE

AT MUSKOGEE, the heart of the Midland Valley and KO&G system, KO&G 803 and Midland Valley 153 (top) were preparing to depart on June 20, 1963. The 153 had been wrecked along with 152 in April 1958 and rebuilt at La Grange as a 1500-h.p. "GP9m." It was crossing the KCS eastward at Pahama (above) on August 28, 1962. At Ft. Smith, the end of the Midland Valley stub, KO&G GP7s 806 and 807 (opposite center and opposite bottom) were idling on June 19, 1963.

The Muskogee Company lines were sold to the Texas & Pacific in September 1964. At that time, the 105 miles of the KO&G from the MoPac crossing at Okay north to Baxter Springs were abandoned, and the Oklahoma City-Ada-Atoka was sold to the Santa Fe. The three names still adorned the herald on the cab of GP7 154 (opposite top left) at Wichita in May 1960. The Midland Valley was merged into the T&P on April 1, 1967, and the KO&G followed suit on April 1, 1970.

MATT HERSON COLLECTION

Jenks Blue

CHAPTER FOUR

THE MISSOURI PACIFIC had been plunged into bankruptcy in 1933 and spent the "Era of the *Eagles*" under the control of Trustee Guy A. Thompson and CEO Lewis W. Baldwin. Following Mr. Baldwin's death in 1946, Paul J. Neff became CEO, and he pursued system dieselization and modernization. On March 1, 1956, the MoPac emerged from the industry's longest bankruptcy (23 years), and Paul Neff was named president. A year later, Neff became chairman of the board, but he died in June 1957, one month after becoming chairman. The presidency went to Russell L. Dearmont, who had served more than 20 years as counsel to the Trustee.

In 1959 the Mississippi River Corporation had begun acquiring stock control of the Missouri Pacific, and it achieved voting control in 1961. The Mississippi River Corporation was a holding company under Chairman William G. Marbury that owned natural gas production and transmission systems and cement industries. Marbury's candidate to replace Mr. Dearmont on the MoPac was Downing B. Jenks, who was president of the Rock Island. When was elected president of the Rock at age 40 in 1956, he was one of the youngest railroad presidents in modern history. Downing B. Jenks became president of the Missouri Pacific on January 16, 1961.

One of Mr. Jenks' first moves was to economize the motive power by simplifying its colorful but complex and expensive-to-apply multi-color paint scheme. The choice was solid dark blue with ScotchLite reflectorized

LOUIS A. MARRE

THE FIRST "JENKS BLUE" repaint, GP7 4169 (above), was at Van Buren, Ark., on June 21, 1961. It was unique in having only one nose chevron. New blue E8 38 (left) and old blue RS3 973 were at St. Louis on New Years Eve 1962.

trim. The "Jenks blue" turned out to be a surprisingly attractive livery. It was first applied to GP7 4169 in June 1961, and the last new units delivered in the old blue and gray were the MoPac 4800-4826 and T&P 1145-1149 GP18s of May 1960.

LOU SCHMITZ COLLECTION

 ## New Colors / Old Numbers

WITH THE STEAM LOCOMOTIVE number series now vacated, the Jenks administration decided in 1962 to rationalize and renumber the diesel fleet, incorporating subsidiaries like T&P and KO&G in the process. Since the Jenks blue had been introduced in June 1961, a few units briefly wore the new blue with the old numbers. About this time, a decision was also made to rid the system of "minority" units, and the entire 145-unit fleet of 1500-h.p. Alco FA1/FB1s and 1600-h.p. FA2/FB2s were slated for trade-in on the next order of GP18s. A few of the 1600-h.p. Alcos briefly wore 1370-series numbers before being retired. Alco FA2 382 (above) was in fresh Jenks blue at North Little Rock on July 10, 1961, in the company of two old-scheme FB2s. The 382 was one of those to be renumbered and saw service as 1382 before being retired by the end of 1962.

A. DEAN HALE

VERY FEW UNITS wore the Jenks blue with their old numbers. Alco PA2 8026 (above) was at Little Rock on July 10, 1961; note the Roman-style numerals in the number board. On that same day, F7 616 (below) and a fresh blue Geep were across the river at North Little Rock. Texas & Pacific E7 2005 (opposite bottom) carried the traditional T&P Gothic number board numerals.

LOUIS A. MARRE

RICHARD R. WALLIN / MATT HERSON COLLECTION

LOU SCHMITZ

Old Colors / New Numbers

THE 1962 RENUMBERING was accomplished much more rapidly than repainting and resulted in most of the fleet wearing new numbers with old colors. Since the FT's were scrapped before renumbering, the oldest F-unit to be renumbered was "class" F3A 513 of November 1947 that became the new 700. The 700 was in the company of F7s 774 and 807 (above) at Kansas City in June 1962. F3A 793 (ex- 574, see page 51) was southbound out of Omaha (left) on October 11, 1963, and F7 813 (below) was at Van Buren in November 1963. F3A 767 (opposite bottom) and an F7B were at Louisville, Ky., in April 1963 while on lease to the power-short Louisville & Nashville. The MoPac units were returned when the L&N bought nine Rutland RS3s!

LOUIS A. MARRE

ST. LOUIS, BROWNSVILLE & MEXICO F7 835 was heading up a perfect A-B-A set (above) at Texarkana in 1962. The same unit had been at North Little Rock (page 103) as the 616 on July 10, 1961. StLB&M 731 (right), at Houston on January 19, 1964, looks like an F7 but is actually a late model F3, originally StLB&M 545, built in June 1948. MoPac Jenks blue 801 (below) had B-units in two liveries rolling through Glendale, Mo., on a coal train on May 22, 1965. StLB&M GP7 205 (opposite center) was leading a pair of T&P F7s out of Ft. Worth in December 1963. MoPac F7 808 (opposite bottom) was departing Omaha on October 13, 1963.

STUART J. SUTTON

A. DEAN HALE

LOU SCHMITZ

ABOVE and BELOW / LOUIS A. MARRE

LOUIS A. MARRE

A. DEAN HALE

THE JENKS BLUE PASSENGER UNITS retained their silver nose eagles. Compare PA2s 57 (opposite top) and 62 (top left center), ex-8014 and 8019, respectively, at North Little Rock on December 31, 1962. Repainted E7 20, formerly 7011, was at the Little Rock passenger station (above) that same day in the company of an old scheme E7. Texas & Pacific F7 924, formerly 1574, and a Jenks blue mate (opposite bottom) were hitting the diamonds at Ft. Worth in March 1964 with a short freight. A nearly perfect T&P A-B-B-A F7 set (below) was at Ft. Worth behind the 886 (formerly 1536) in December 1962. The T&P F7s had dynamic brakes, evidenced by the fifth topside fan. The third unit is a MoPac F7B, lacking the dynamic brake fan.

A. DEAN HALE

Transition in Texas and Oklahoma

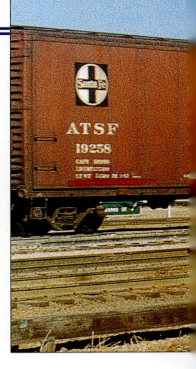

A. DEAN HALE

ONE OF THE FOUR KO&G F7 cab units, delivered in MoPac blue and gray (page 95) had been repainted Jenks blue while retaining its rectangular three-name herald (above) as it followed old-scheme MoPac F7 802 through Ft. Worth in 1964.

NEW NUMBERS WERE APPLIED to more "old" liveries than just the MoPac blue and gray. Texas & Pacific swamp holly orange GP7 1118 became 118 and was working at Ft. Worth (above right) in August 1961 with MP 266, the former I-GN 4287. KO&G GP7 804 had lost its cab herald and had been renumbered 100 (opposite center) when it was at Ft. Worth in May 1965 working with Jenks blue T&P GP7 129, the former orange 1129. Midland Valley 154 (page 97) had been renumbered 107 (below) as it moved through Tulsa in June 1964. KO&G GP7 807 (page 98) was at Texarkana in April 1968 (opposite bottom left) as 103 with MoPac herald and KO&G sublettering. The 104 (opposite bottom right), at Abilene on February 13, 1973, was lettered "TP."

EMERY GULASH / MORNING SUN BOOKS COLLECTION

ABOVE and BELOW / A. DEAN HALE

JIM BOYD   ALLAN RAMSEY / PETER ARNOLD COLLECTION

A Second-Hand E8

AL HOLTZ

THE PASSENGER BUSINESS was still a major part of MoPac and T&P operations in the early 1960s. In June 1962 the MoPac bought Boston & Maine 3821, its one and only E8. It was at Charlestown, Mass., in July 1956 (above) with railfan photographer Walt Zullig chatting with the engineer. The B&M unit became MoPac 42 and was given the Jenks blue livery. A Mars light was put in the top nose housing, and a new nose door with a headlight was installed. The 42 was at St. Louis Union Station (opposite top) on October 3, 1965. In November 1969 (opposite bottom) it was on the *Missouri River Eagle* at Kansas City Union Station (opposite bottom). In September 1970 it was showing fresh paint (below) and attentive maintenance at St. Louis Union Station. When Amtrak arrived on May 1, 1971, the MoPac was down to two trains each way between St. Louis and Kansas City and one each way between St. Louis and Texarkana.

STEVE BOGEN

MATT HERSON COLLECTION

T.J. DONAHUE

LOUIS A. MARRE

 ## Jenks Blue with a Different Slant

THIS IS PURELY PERSONAL. I have always regarded Electro-Motive's slant-nosed E-units to be the most elegant diesel machines in railroading, and the Jenks blue emphasized their sleek lines extraordinarily well. The MoPac had five slant-noses, but only the two E6s survived into the blue era. E3s 7000 and 7001 and AA6 7100 were scrapped in early 1962 and were never assigned new numbers. E6 7003, however, was at North Little Rock (above) on July 10, 1961, awaiting new paint and number 12. Sister 7002 was at St. Louis (below) as No. 11 on Leap Year February 29, 1964, and a few months later (opposite top) at Kansas City. One of my most frustrating moments came at St. Louis in 1964 when an E6 slid out of the far side of Union Station (opposite center) and then hid in the engine shed. I was the only time I ever saw one.

LOUIS A. MARRE

LOUIS A. MARRE

JIM BOYD

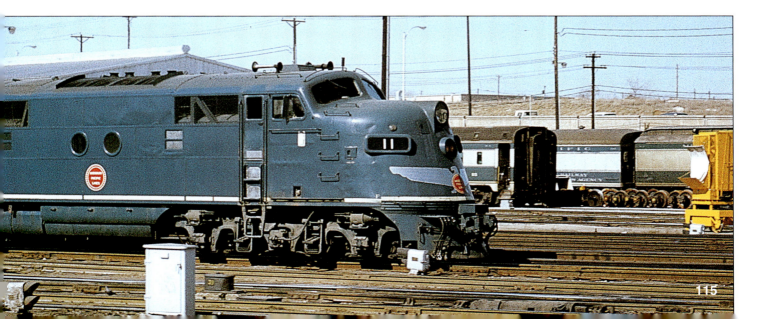

THE FIRST ALCO on the Missouri-Illinois was RS2 61 (page 71) in November 1949, following a single EMD NW2 in July 1949. Between January 1951 and March 1955, the M-I replaced steam with 13 1600-h.p. RS3s. The Alco fleet was renumbered 960-973 in 1962. The 965 (below) was in factory livery at Dupo in February 1963, while the 972 (right) was at North Little Rock on December 31, 1962, beside MoPac 974 (page 121). The 971 (above) was at Mitchell, Ill, in September 1964. The 964 (bottom), at St. Louis in December 1963, carried "MI" under the herald.

FOUR PHOTOS / LOUIS A. MARRE

The Amazing "Mike & Ike"

THE MISSOURI-ILLINOIS RAILROAD was created on July 1, 1929, when the MoPac combined a lead-mining short line in Missouri and an 82-mile railroad between the B&O at Salem, Ill., and the Mississippi River at Kellogg. Using the steel-hulled side-wheel carferry *Ste. Genevieve* to cross the river, the M-I formed a bypass route around the south side of St. Louis (right). The 1922-built *Ste. Genevieve* (below) was worked by M-I Alcos before it was retired in June 1961.

MISSOURI PACIFIC PHOTO

OFFICIAL GUIDE OF THE RAILWAYS / NOVEMBER 1951

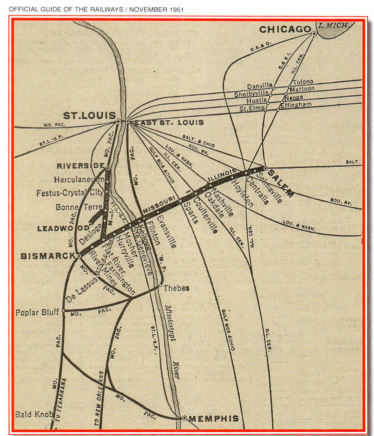

MAC OWEN COLLECTION

JIM BOYD

J. DAVID INGLES / MATT HERSON COLLECTION

TP-MP TERMINAL of New Orleans rostered three RS2s (21-23, re# 956-958); the 957 (top) was at New Orleans in January 1966. The Missouri-Illinois' sole RS2, 960, was at Valley Junction, Ill., (above) in 1964 with Illinois Central 702, on of the three ex-Peabody Short Line RS2s. MoPac RS3s 990 and 991 (opposite top) were fresh from the North Little Rock paint shop on New Years Eve 1962. MoPac 992 and 998 (opposite bottom) were kicking out typical 244-engine smoke at Kansas City on July 14, 1966. RS11 4606, repainted Jenks blue and renumbered 949 (right), was at St. Louis in September 1964.

Blue Alco Road Switchers

ABOVE and BELOW / LOUIS A. MARRE

THREE PHOTOS / JIM BOYD

IN THE PRE-DAWN GLOW, Missouri-Illinois RS2 965 (top) paused on the eastward descent from the MacArthur Bridge with the still-incomplete Gateway Arch in the distance. As the light came up, the train began to move (above) down over the quiet streets of East St. Louis, where the only other activity was police cars rounding up the drunks and ladies of the night. The 965 (opposite bottom) was working 23rd Street Yard near Union Station later that day. MoPac RS3 974 (opposite top) was at North Little Rock on December 31, 1962. Note the "F" on the short hood frame.

LOUIS A. MARRE

Missouri Pacific Capsule History

MISSOURI PACIFIC PUBLIC TIMETABLE / JULY 7, 1946

IN THE "ERA BEFORE THE *EAGLES*" the premier passenger train on the Missouri Pacific was the *Sunshine Limited* with sections from St. Louis to El Paso, Texas, and to Mexico City via San Antonio. It survived even past the introduction of the *Texas Eagle*.

THE PACIFIC RAILROAD, the first to be built west of the Mississippi River, struck out west from St. Louis on July 4, 1851, on 5-foot 6-inch gauge track, supremely confident that the mighty Mississippi would never be bridged. The Rock Island crossed the river into Iowa five years later, and the Union Pacific transcontinental railroad was built to standard gauge. The Pacific Railroad reached Kansas City in 1865 and was probing westward toward Omaha when the Eads Bridge was completed to bring the Eastern standard gauge systems into St. Louis. The entire Pacific Railroad was standard gauged in 14 hours on July 18, 1869. Its name was changed to Missouri Pacific Railway in 1876.

In 1858 the St. Louis & Iron Mountain was opened from St. Louis 86 miles southward to the iron mining region at Pilot Knob, Missouri. Over the next dozen years the StL&IM reached southeast to a ferry connection with the Mobile & Ohio between Belmont, Mo., and Columbus, Ky., and southward to the Arkansas state line below Poplar Bluff, Missouri. The St. Louis, Iron Mountain & Southern was created in 1874 the StL&IM merged with the Cairo & Fulton, that had built from the west bank of the Mississippi River at Birds Point, Mo., near Cairo, Ill., to a connection with the Texas & Pacific at Texarkana. That year the T&P had completed its routes from Shreveport, La., and Texarkana to Dallas, Texas.

The International & Great Northern was chartered in 1873 to consolidate lines from the T&P at Longview south to Houston and Galveston and to create a line to the Mexican border at Laredo.

Financier Jay Gould acquired control of the Missouri Pacific in 1879 and soon added to his "family" the St. Louis, Iron Mountain & Southern; the I&GN; the Missouri, Kansas & Texas; the Wabash and the Union Pacific. Under Gould, the MoPac was extended north to Omaha and west from Kansas City of Pueblo, Colorado. The T&P became the second transcontinental railroad when Gould pushed it westward from Ft. Worth to Sierra Blanca, Texas, to link up with the eastward-reaching Southern Pacific on December 15, 1881, to create a through route to California. A year later the T&P purchased lines and built new track to reach New Orleans in September 1882.

Gould went too far too fast, however, and in rapid succession beginning in 1884, the Wabash, T&P, MK&T and I&GN went bankrupt. The Missouri Pacific Railway and StLIM&S were merged as the Missouri Pacific Railroad in 1917. While others were spun off, the T&P and I&GN stayed with the Missouri Pacific. By the 1920s the Gould chaos was being sorted out. The I&GN was reorganized as the International-Great Northern and joined with the Gulf Coast Lines, comprised of the New Orleans, Texas & Mexico and the St. Louis, Brownsville & Mexico. The MoPac took control of the Gulf Coast Lines in 1924 and the Texas & Pacific in 1930, but to accommodate Texas laws, the subsidiaries retained their individual identities.

In the Great Depression, the MoPac entered a bankruptcy in 1933 from which it did not emerge until March 1, 1956. This became the longest receivership in railroad history.

MISSOURI PACIFIC FT 507 heads up a power set at St. Louis on November 24, 1945.

Rosters and Maps

Missouri Pacific System Units Retired Before 1962 Renumbering

Number	RR	Model.	Builder	Built	Retired	Notes
201-208	MP	DR4-4-1500A	Baldwin	11-12/48	9/57	"Babyface;" boiler equipped; 1500-h.p. 8-cyl. 608SC
201B-204B	MP	DR4-4-1500B	Baldwin	11-12/48	9/57	Booster; 1500-h.p. 8-cyl. 608SC engine
301-330	MP	FA1	Alco-GE	3/48-6/50	1961-;62	Cab unit; 1500-h.p. 12-cyl. 244 engine
301B-310B	MP	FB1	Alco-GE	3-4/48	1961-'62	Booster; 1500-h.p. 12-cyl. 244 engine
321B-325B	MP	FB1	Alco-GE	5-6/50	1961-'62	Booster; 1500-h.p. 12-cyl. 244 engine
331-360	MP	FA2	Alco-GE	4/51-1/52	1961-'62	Cab unit; 1600-h.p. 12-cyl. 244 engine
331B-335B	MP	FB2	Alco-GE	4/51	1962	Booster unit; 1600-h.p. 12-cyl. 244 engine
345B-356B	MP	FB2	Alco-GE	12/51-1/52	1962	Booster unit; 1600-h.p. 12-cyl. 244 engine
361-373	MP	FPA2	Alco-GE	1/52-853	1961-'62	Cab unit; boiler equipped; 1600-h.p. 12-cyl. 244 engine
370B-392B	MP	FB2	Alco-GE	6/53-4/54	1962	Booster unit; 1600-h.p. 12-cyl. 244 engine
374-386	MP	FA2	Alco-GE	6/53-3/54	1961-;62	Cab unit; 1600-h.p. 12-cyl. 244 engine
387-392	MP	FPA2	Alco-GE	3-4/54	1962	Cab unit; boiler equipped; 1600-h.p. 12-cyl. 244 engine
501-512	MP	FTA	EMD	11/43-7/45	1960	Cab unit; 1350-h.p. 16-cyl 567 engine
501B-512B	MP	FTB	EMD	11/43-7/45	1960	Booster; 501B-504B drawbars; 505B-512B couplers
528; 526B	IGN	F3A, F3B	EMD	11/47	Pre-1962	Cab and booster; retired before re#
803	MP	DE-44	Dav-Bessler	10/40	9/57	44-ton, 350-h.p., twin Hercules DFXD 6-cyl. engines
805-807	MP	44DE22	Whitcomb	10-12/41	1957-'58	44-ton, 350-h.p., twin Hercules DFXD 6-cyl. engines
805-807	MP	44DE22	Whitcomb	10-12/41	1957-'58	44-ton, 350-h.p., twin Hercules DFXD 6-cyl. engines
805-807	MP	44DE22	Whitcomb	10-12/41	1957-'58	44-ton, 350-h.p., twin Hercules DFXD 6-cyl. engines
808-810	MP	DE-44	Dav-Bessler	12/41-1/42	1956-'57	44-ton, 350-h.p., twin Hercules DFXD 6-cyl. engines
812	IGN	44-Tonner	GE	1/42	4/56	44-ton, 350-h.p., twin Hercules DFXD 6-cyl. engines
813	StLB&M	44-Tonner	GE	1/42	4/56	44-ton, 350-h.p., twin Hercules DFXD 6-cyl. engines
815	BSL&W	44-Tonner	GE	1/42	4/58	44-ton, 350-h.p., twin Hercules DFXD 6-cyl. engines
2917	NO&LC	DLC	Plymouth	10/26	1935	63-h.p. gas-mechanical
3002	NO&LC	JLA	Plymouth	5/35	4/59	12-ton, 100-h.p. gas-mechanical
4100-4101	MP	NC2	EMC	7/37	5/61, 12/60	900-h.p. V-12 Winton 201A engine
4102-4103	MP	NW4	EMC	8/38	2-3/61	Ex-EMC 823, 824; 900-h.p. V-12 201A; boiler eqpt.
4104-4111	MP	BL2	EMD	5-9/48	1962	"Branch Line" 1500-h.p. V-16 567B
4112-4115	StLB&M	DRS4-4-1500	Baldwin	2/49	Pre-1962	1500-h.p. 608SC turbocharged inline 8-cyl. engine
4195-4196	I-GN	AS16	BLH	11/51	Pre-1962	1600-h.p. 608A turbocharged inline 8-cyl. engine
4208, 4236	MP	GP7	EMD	2/52	5/60	Wrecked, traded; EMD 1500-h.p. V-16 567B engine
7000-7001	MP	E3A	EMC	10/39	5/62	2000-h.p., twin 1000-h.p. V-12 567 engines
7100	MP	AA6	EMC	8/40	2/62	EMC's last "motor car." One 1000-h.p. V-12 567 engine.
9001	MP	SC	EMC	7/37	Sold 12/59	600-h.p. Winton 201A; to Dardenelle & Russellville 14.
9010	MP	VO660	Baldwin	8/40	Sold 6/59	660-h.p. 6-cyl. VO engine; to Witt Gravel, to Parish Line
9105	MP	NW2	EMD	8/40	1/60	1000-h.p. V-12 567 engine
9149	StLB&M	DS4-4-1000	Baldwin	3/50	1/62	1000-h.p. 606SC turbocharged engine
9201	I-GN	SW1	EMC	12/39	12/59	600-h.p. V-6 567; re# 9017
9206	SAU&G	SW1	EMD	6/41	Sold 3/59	600-h.p. V-6 567; re# 9022; to Georgetown RR 1000

Missouri Pacific System 1962 Renumbering

1962 No.	RR	Original No.	Model	Built	Notes
1-10	T&P	2000-2009	E7A	1947-'49	EMD 2000-h.p. twin 1000-h.p. V-12 567A engines
11-12	MP	7002-7003	E6A	1941	EMD 2000-h.p. twin 1000-h.p. V-12 567 engines
11B-12B	MP	7002B-7003B	E6B	1941	Booster. EMD 2000-h.p. twin 1000-h.p. V-12 567 engines
13-26	MP	7004-7017	E7A	1947-'48	IGN 7007, 7012, 7013; StLB&M 7008, 7009
13B-21B	MP	7004B-7917B	E7B	1947-'49	Booster. IGN 7012B; 2000-h.p. twin V-12 567A engines
30-37	T&P	2010-2017	E8A	1951	EMD 2250-h.p. twin 1125-h.p. V-12 567B engines
38-41	MP	7018-7021	E8A	1950	EMD 2250-h.p. twin 1125-h.p. V-12 567B engines
42	MP	B&M 3821	E8A	1950	Purchased 6/62; EMD 2250-h.p. twin V-12 567B engines
44-51	MP	8001-8008	PA1	1949	Alco 2000-h.p. 244C V-16 engine
52-61	MP	8009-8018	PA2	1951	Alco 2250-h.p. 244C V-16 engine
62-79	MP	8019-8036	PA3	1952	Alco 2250-h.p. 244D V-16 engine
97-105	KO&G	801-809	GP7	1952-'53	To T&P 9/64; EMD 1500-h.p. V-16 567B engine
106-109	MV	151, 154, 152-153	GP7	1953	To T&P 9/64; 152-153 wrecked and rebuilt to GP9m 4/58
110-130	T&P	1110-1130	GP7	1950-'52	EMD 1500-h.p. V-16 567B engine
131-135	StLB&M	4116-4120	GP7	1950	EMD 1500-h.p. V-16 567B engine
136-138	IGN	4121-4123	GP7	1950	EMD 1500-h.p. V-16 567B engine
139-156	MP	4124-4141	GP7	1950	EMD 1500-h.p. V-16 567B engine
157-162	IGN	4153-4158	GP7	1951	Boiler equipped; EMD 1500-h.p. V-16 567B engine
163-164	StLB&M	4159-4160	GP7	1951	Boiler equipped; EMD 1500-h.p. V-16 567B engine
165-166	StLB&M	4164-4165	GP7	1951	Boiler equipped; EMD 1500-h.p. V-16 567B engine
167-195	MP	4166-4194	GP7	1951	EMD 1500-h.p. V-16 567B engine
196-201	IGN	4197-4202	GP7	1952	EMD 1500-h.p. V-16 567B engine
202-206	StLB&M	4203-4207	GP7	1952	EMD 1500-h.p. V-16 567B engine
207-233	MP	4209-4235	GP7	1952	EMD 1500-h.p. V-16 567B engine
234-237	MP	4237-4240	GP7	1952	EMD 1500-h.p. V-16 567B engine
239	StLB&M	4249	GP7	1952	Boiler equipped; EMD 1500-h.p. V-16 567B engine
240-262	MP	4261-4283	GP7	1953	EMD 1500-h.p. V-16 567B engine
263-265	StLB&M	4284-4286	GP7	1953	EMD 1500-h.p. V-16 567B engine
266-276	IGN	4287-4297	GP7	1953-'54	EMD 1500-h.p. V-16 567B engine
277	StLB&M	4298	GP7	1954	EMD 1500-h.p. V-16 567B engine
278-294	MP	4299-4315	GP7	1954	EMD 1500-h.p. V-16 567B engine
295-305	MP	4142-4152	GP7	1950-'51	Boiler equipped; EMD 1500-h.p. V-16 567B engine
306-308	StLB&M	4161-4163	GP7	1951	Boiler equipped; EMD 1500-h.p. V-16 567B engine
309-315	MP	4241-4248	GP7	1952	Boiler equipped; EMD 1500-h.p. V-16 567B engine
316-317	StLB&M	4250-4251	GP7	1952	Boiler equipped; EMD 1500-h.p. V-16 567B engine
318-319	StLB&M	4252-4253	GP7	1953	Boiler equipped; EMD 1500-h.p. V-16 567B engine
320-321	IGN	4254-4255	GP7	1953	Boiler equipped; EMD 1500-h.p. V-16 567B engine
322-326	MP	4256-4260	GP7	1953	Boiler equipped; EMD 1500-h.p. V-16 567B engine
327-333	MP	4316-4322	GP7	1954	Boiler equipped; EMD 1500-h.p. V-16 567B engine
334-334	StLB&M	4323-4324	GP7	1954	Boiler equipped; EMD 1500-h.p. V-16 567B engine
335	IGN	4325	GP7	1954	Boiler equipped; EMD 1500-h.p. V-16 567B engine
346-385	MP	4332-4371	GP9	1955	EMD 1750-h.p. V-16 567C engine
386-391	T&P	1131-1136	GP9	1957	EMD 1750-h.p. V-16 567C engine
392-399	T&P	1137-1144	GP9	1957	Dynamic brakes; EMD 1750-h.p. V-16 567C engine
505-528	MP	4801-4824	GP18	1960-'62	High short hood; EMD 1750-h.p. V-16 567C engine
700-711	MP	513-524	F3A	11/47	EMD 1500-h.p. V-16 567B engine
712-714	IGN	525-527	F3A	11/47	EMD 1500-h.p. V-16 567B engine
715-738	StLB&M	529-552	F3A	11/47-6/48	EMD 1500-h.p. V-16 567B engine
739-746	IGN	553-560	F5A	9/48	EMD 1500-h.p. V-16 567B engine
765-770	MP	561-566	F3A	8/48	Boiler equipped; EMD 1500-h.p. V-16 567B engine
771-774	MP	567-570	F5A	9/48	Boiler equipped; EMD 1500-h.p. V-16 567B engine
785-786	IGN	617-618	F7A	4/50	Boiler equipped; EMD 1500-h.p. V-16 567B engine
790-795	MP	571-576	F3A	8/48	EMD 1500-h.p. V-16 567B engine
796-813	MP	577-594	F7A	9-10/49	EMD 1500-h.p. V-16 567B engine
814-821	IGN	595-602	F7A	9/49	EMD 1500-h.p. V-16 567B engine
822-825	IGN	603-606	F7A	9/49	Boiler equipped; EMD 1500-h.p. V-16 567B engine
826-835	StLB&M	607-616	F7A	10/49-4/50	611-614 boiler equipped; EMD 1500-h.p. V-16 567B engine
836-843	MP	619-626	F7A	3/51	EMD 1500-h.p. V-16 567B engine
790B-795B	MP	513B-518B	F3B	11/47	EMD 1500-h.p. V-16 567B engine
796B	IGN	525B	F3B	11/47	EMD 1500-h.p. V-16 567B engine
801B-806B	MP	561B-566B	F3B	8/48	Boiler equipped; EMD 1500-h.p. V-16 567B engine
807B-810B	MP	567B-570B	F5B	9/48	Boiler equipped; EMD 1500-h.p. V-16 567B engine
811B-818B	MP	587B-594B	F7B	10/49	EMD 1500-h.p. V-16 567B engine
819B-820B	IGN	595B-596B	F7B	9/49	EMD 1500-h.p. V-16 567B engine
821B-822B	MP	619B-620B	F7B	3/51	EMD 1500-h.p. V-16 567B engine
844-847	KO&G	751-754	F7A	4/49	Delivered in MP/T&P freight livery; to T&P 9/64

1962 No.	RR	Original No.	Model	Built	Notes
846B-847B	KO&G	755B-756B	F7B	4/49	Delivered in MP/T&P freight livery; to T&P 9/64
850, 851	T&P	1500, 1501	F7A	2/49, 11/49	Boiler equipped, *Eagle* livery; dynamic brakes
850B, 851B	T&P	1500B, 1501B	F7B	2/49, 11/49	*Eagle* livery; dynamic brakes; 1500-h.p. V-16 567B engine
852-930	T&P	1502-1580	F7A	11/49-8/51	Dynamic brakes; EMD 1500-h.p. V-16 567B engine
852B-880B	T&P	1502B-1530B	F7B	11/49-7/51	Dynamic brakes; EMD 1500-h.p. V-16 567B engine
881B-884B	T&P	1531B-1534B	F7B	1/52	Boiler equipped, *Eagle* livery; dynamic brakes
931-932	T&P	1581-1582	F7A	8/51	Boiler equipped, *Eagle* livery; dynamic brakes
935-940	STLB&M	4326-4331	AS16	6-7/54	Baldwin-Lima-Hamilton; re# 941-946, then 935-940
944-955	MP	4601-4612	RS11	10-11/59	Alco, 1800-h.p. V-12. 251; on Baldwin Babyface trucks
956-958	TPMPT	21-23	RS2	4/48-1/49	Alco, 1500-h.p. 12-cyl. 244 engine; 23 delivered as 1100
959	TPMPT	24	RS3	4/56	Alco, 1600-h.p. 12-cyl. 244 engine
960	M-I	61	RS2	11/49	Alco, 1500-h.p. 12-cyl. 244 engine
961-973	M-I	62-74	RS3	1/51-3/55	Alco, 1600-h.p. 12-cyl. 244 engine
974-999	MP	4501-4526	RS3	1-2/55	Alco, 1600-h.p. 12-cyl. 244 engine
1000-1019	T&P	1000-1019	NW2	11/46-5/49	EMD, 1000-h.p. 12-cyl. 567 engine
1020	FWB	2	NW2	10/46	EMD, 1000-h.p. 12-cyl. 567 engine
1021, 1022	MP	9104, 9106	NW2	9/39, 8/41	EMC, EMD, 1000-h.p. 12-cyl. 567 engine
1023	MP	9000	SC	7/37	EMC, 600-h.p. 8-cyl. Winton 201A; repowered by EMD 8/62
1027, 1028	KO&G, M-I	1001, 51	NW2	5/49, 7/49	EMD, 1000-h.p. 12-cyl. 567 engine; 1027 to T&P 9/64
1035	MP	9102	HH1000	9/39	Alco, High-hood, 1000-h.p. 6-cyl. 539 engine
1036-1045	MP	9107-9116	S2	8/41-5/45	Alco, 1000-h.p. 6-cyl. 539 engine
1046-1050	MP	9128-9132	S2	5-10/49	Alco, 1000-h.p. 6-cyl. 539 engine
1051-1053	IGN	9156-9158	S2	9-10/45	Alco, 1000-h.p. 6-cyl. 539 engine
1054	StLB&M	9159	S2	5/46	Alco, 1000-h.p. 6-cyl. 539 engine
1055-1056	IGN	9168-9169	S2	7/49	Alco, 1000-h.p. 6-cyl. 539 engine
1057-1060	TPMPT	11-14	S2	3-5/48	Alco, 1000-h.p. 6-cyl. 539 engine
1062	MP	9103	VO1000	10/39	Baldwin, 1000-h.p. 8-cyl. VO engine
1063-1065	MP	9117-9119	VO1000	3-7/45	Baldwin, 1000-h.p. 8-cyl. VO engine
1066-1073	MP	9120-9127	DS4-4-1000SC	2/45-3/49	Baldwin, 1000-h.p. 6-cyl. 606SC turbochargd engine
1074-1082	MP	9133-9141	DS4-4-1000SC	3-4/50	Baldwin, 1000-h.p. 6-cyl. 606SC turbochargd engine
1083, --	StLB&M	9148, 9149	DS4-4-1000SC	3/50	Baldwin, 1000-h.p. 6-cyl. 606SC; 9149 retired before re#
1089-1091	StLB&M	9155, 9160-61	VO1000	3/44	Baldwin, 1000-h.p. 8-cyl. VO engine
1092-1097	StLB&M	9162-9167	DS4-4-1000SC	3/49	Baldwin, 1000-h.p. 6-cyl. 606SC turbochargd engine
1098-1099	URM	9198-9199	VO1000	4/46	Baldwin, 1000-h.p. 8-cyl. VO engine
1210-1214	MP	9142-9146	SW7	6/50	EMD, 1200-h.p. 12-cyl. 567A engine
1215-1218	T&P	1020-1023	SW7	7/50	EMD, 1200-h.p. 12-cyl. 567A engine
1219-1231	T&P	1024-1036	SW9	2-8/51	EMD, 1200-h.p. 12-cyl. 567B engine
1232-1248	MP	9170-9186	SW9	4/51	EMD, 1200-h.p. 12-cyl. 567B engine
1249-1253	StLB&M	9187-9191	SW9	4/51	EMD, 1200-h.p. 12-cyl. 567B engine
1260-1286	MP	9200-9226	S12	5/51-4/52	Baldwin, 1200-h.p. 6-cyl. 606A turbocharged engine
1287-1289	StLB&M	9227-9229	S12	4/52	Baldwin, 1200-h.p. 6-cyl. 606A turbocharged engine
1290-1292	IGN	9230-9232	S12	4/52	Baldwin, 1200-h.p. 6-cyl. 606A turbocharged engine
1293-1299	UT	9233-9239	S12	4-5/53	Baldwin, 1200-h.p. 6-cyl. 606A turbocharged engine
1650	NO&LC	3003	JDT	8/57	Plymouth 18-ton gas-mechanical
2400	NO&LC	3000	ML-6	6/31	Plymouth 30-ton gas-mechanical
3004	NO&LC	MP 2401--	JDT	4/61	Plymouth 25-ton, 240-h.p. gas-mech.; Cont. Grain 2401
3500-3502	MP	800-801, 811	44-Tonner	2/41, 1/42	GE 44-ton 350-h.p. twin Hercules 6-cyl. DFXD engines
3503	STLB&M	814	44-Tonner	1/42	GE 44-ton 350-h.p. twin Hercules 6-cyl. DFXD engines
3504	MP	802	44-Ton	2/41	Porter 44-ton 350-h.p. twin Hercules 6-cyl. DFXD engines
3505	MP	804	44DE-6	11/40	Whitcomb 44-ton 350-h.p. twin Hercules DFXD engines
6005, 6006	UT	5, 10	SW	5/38, 12/38	EMC 600-h.p. Winton 8-cyl. 201A; interim SJB 5 and 10
6007	MP	9002	SC	7/37	EMC 600-h.p. Winton 8-cyl. 201A; interim SJB 2 then 11
6008	SJB	12	SW1	4/47	EMD 600-h.p. 6-cyl. 567 engine
6009	MP	9003	SC	7/37	EMC 600-h.p. Winton 8-cyl. 201A engine
6010-6013	MP	9004-06, 9011	SW1	9/39-8/41	EMC 600-h.p. 6-cyl. 567 engine
6014-6017	IGN	9200, 9202-04	SW1	12/39-6/41	EMC 600-h.p. 6-cyl. 567 engine; interim 9016-9019
6018	FWB	1	SW1	1/39	EMC 600-h.p. 6-cyl. 567 engine
6600-6601	MP	9007-9008	S1	10/40	Alco, 600-h.p. 6-cyl. 539 engine
6602, 6603	TPMPT	2, 3	S1	11/40, 8/41	Alco, 600-h.p. 6-cyl. 539 engine
6604-6606	NO&LC	9013-9015	S1	10-11/47	Alco, 600-h.p. 6-cyl. 539 engine
6610-6611	URM	9090-9091	VO660	3/42	Baldwin 660-h.p. 6-cyl. VO engine
6612, 6613	MP	9009, 9012	VO660	8/40, 7/41	Baldwin 660-h.p. 6-cyl. VO engine
9021	IGN	9205	SW1	6/41	EMD, 600-h.p. V-6 567

RAILROAD ABBREVIATIONS: B&M Boston & Maine; **FWB** Ft. Worth Belt; **KO&G** Kansas, Oklahoma & Gulf; **MV** Midland Valley; **M-I** Missouri-Illinois; **MP** Missouri Pacific; **NO&LC** New Orleans & Lower Coast; **SJB** St. Joseph Belt; **T&P** Texas & Pacific; **TPMPT** Texas Pacific-Missouri Pacific Terminal Railroad of New Orleans; **URM** Union Railway (Memphis); **UT** Union Terminal Railway (St. Joseph).

MISSOURI PACIFIC MARCH 18, 1951, PUBLIC TIMETABLE

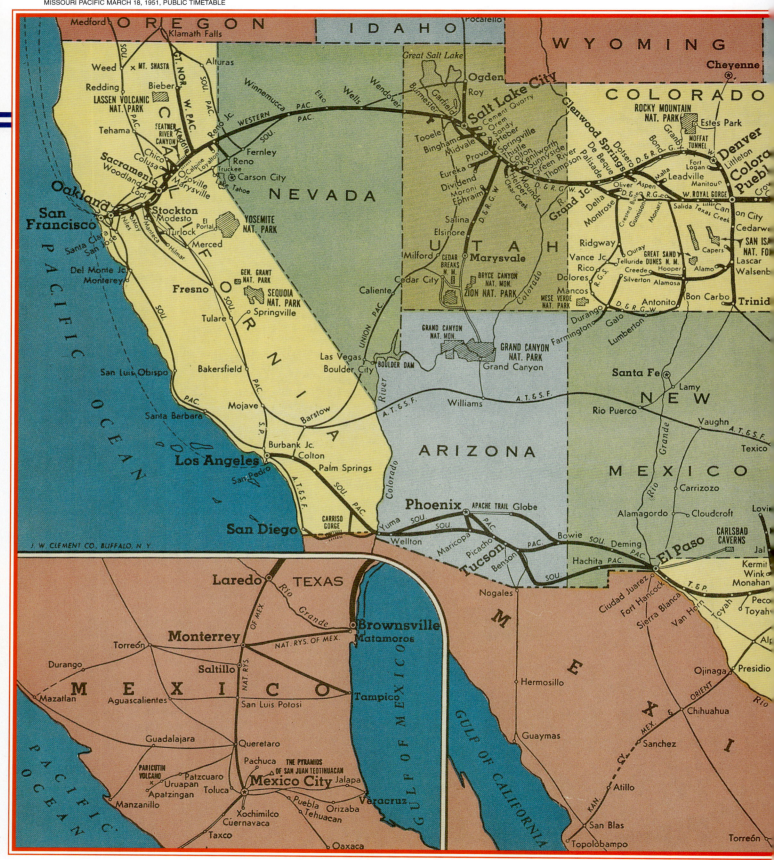

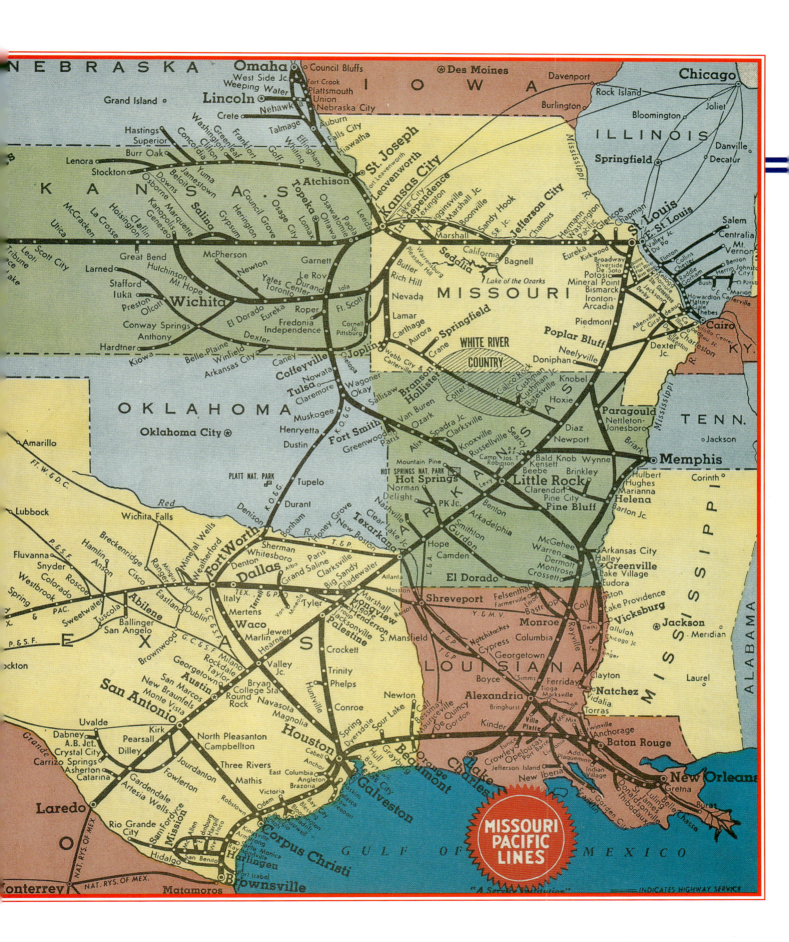

"SCREAMIN' EAGLES" adorned the long hood of new SD40s at Texarkana in March 1968. The C&EI was in transition (bottom left) at Yard Center in Dolton, Ill., in 1967 with FP7 1602 in C&EI livery and 1605 wearing the MoPac herald. SD40-2 3227 (bottom right) wore the MP name on UP colors at Grimsby, Ill., on the Benton line on August 30, 1986.

Epilogue

PREVIEW: SCREAMIN' EAGLES

MISSOURI PACIFIC IN COLOR, Volume 2, **Screamin' Eagles,** from Morning Sun Books, will pick up where this book leaves off, in the 1960s with the first low-nose GP18s, the 1962 renumbering and the arrival of the first turbocharged units with the "Screamin' Eagle" herald on their sides. It will also include the Chicago & Eastern Illinois merger in 1967, the Alton & Southern deal of 1968, the image change and horsepower renumbering of 1974 and the transitioning into the Union Pacific in 1982.

The book will focus on new locomotive deliveries, disposition of retired units and repowering of the Alcos. It will also show pre-Amtrak passenger action at New Orleans, Ft. Worth, St. Louis, Kansas City and Omaha as the Missouri Pacific played out its last glory years and finalized its place in the history books.